Design Patterns

For Scalable and Maintainable

Software

Design Patterns

For Scalable and Maintainable Software

Vinu V Das

Tabor Press

ISBN: 978-1-997541-09-7

Table of Contents

Chapter 1: Introduction to Design Patterns

Software systems have grown remarkably complex, demanding solutions that are not only functional but also robust, adaptable, and scalable. As codebases expand and become increasingly interdependent, the challenges of maintaining clarity, flexibility, and efficiency grow exponentially. This is where design patterns come into play—long-established, battle-tested approaches to solving recurring design problems in a systematic, consistent, and reusable way.

1.1 What Are Design Patterns?

Design patterns are succinctly described as **proven solutions to common, recurring design problems in software development.** They exist at a level of abstraction above raw code, offering a blueprint for how to tackle a particular issue effectively. While patterns provide guidance, they are not direct code snippets you can plug into an application without thought; rather, they serve as adaptable frameworks that you shape to match specific project requirements.

Understanding the Concept

At a conceptual level, each design pattern addresses a well-defined problem that arises again and again in the domain of software design. By formalizing a well-vetted solution, patterns save engineers from reinventing the wheel. For instance, consider the challenge of ensuring a class in your application has only one global instance: the well-known **Singleton Pattern** outlines an approach to achieve this with thread safety and controlled access.

Because patterns can be mixed, matched, and modified, they offer a wide tapestry of potential solutions. This flexibility is particularly important in modern development, where distributed systems, microservices, mobile applications, and monolithic back-ends might coexist. Patterns are therefore recognized as **language-agnostic**—although certain implementations may take advantage of features in languages like Java, C++, Python, or JavaScript, the underlying ideas are generally transferrable to any object-oriented or even multi-paradigm environment.

Defining Characteristics

To better internalize the idea of design patterns, consider the following core characteristics that are often present in each pattern:

1. **Reusability**: A design pattern is crafted based on repeated success in multiple contexts. If a solution has been validated in many scenarios, it qualifies for pattern status.

2. **Abstraction**: Patterns typically describe how to solve a problem at a conceptual or structural level. While code examples can illustrate implementations, the pattern itself remains an abstract guide.

3. **Language** Independence: Because patterns capture an approach rather than specific language constructs, they can be applied across diverse programming languages and ecosystems.

4. **Problem-Solving Nature:** Patterns zero in on a particular type of problem—for example, how to create objects without specifying the exact class (Factory Method), or how to decouple sending and receiving objects (Observer).

5. **Shared Vocabulary:** Each pattern is a named construct—like "Factory Method," "Observer," or "Decorator." This naming convention fosters a concise language for discussing design ideas among developers.

Real-World Analogies

A real-world analogy for design patterns is the concept of **blueprints** or **recipes** in construction and cooking. For instance, a builder might have a standard set of blueprints for a small office layout that can be adapted and expanded. Similarly, in cooking, a recipe for a basic sauce can be tweaked for variations. In software, once you recognize that a particular arrangement of classes or methods consistently solves a problem—like handling user subscriptions to an event—it can be replicated wherever that problem recurs.

The Concept of a Design Pattern

Below is a simplified diagram that illustrates how design patterns occupy an abstract level guiding multiple categories.

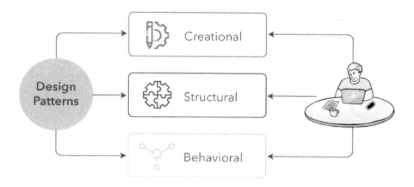

Figure 1: High-level depiction of design patterns as an abstract concept, branching into main types.

1.2 History and Evolution of Design Patterns

While design patterns might seem intrinsically connected to software, the seeds of this idea were first planted in the field of architecture. Recognizing the cross-disciplinary roots of patterns underscores their universality and adaptive potential.

The Architectural Roots

The lineage of design patterns can be traced to Christopher Alexander, an architect whose groundbreaking work in the 1970s—most notably *A Pattern Language*—inspired the broader concept of codifying best practices. Alexander noticed that certain design solutions in architecture and urban planning recurred so often that they deserved names and structured descriptions. This allowed architects to communicate these solutions more effectively and reuse them in different contexts.

In the decades that followed, forward-thinking software pioneers realized that complex software systems, much like buildings and urban spaces, faced recurring problems that begged for a standardized set of solutions.

Emergence in Software Engineering

It wasn't until the late 1980s and early 1990s that the software community began to embrace this pattern-based thinking. Ward Cunningham and Kent Beck experimented with adapting Alexander's ideas to object-oriented programming. However, the true inflection point came in 1994 with the publication of the seminal work *Design Patterns: Elements of Reusable Object-Oriented Software* by Erich Gamma, Richard Helm, Ralph Johnson, and John Vlissides, commonly referred to as the **Gang of Four (GoF)**.

The GoF book introduced 23 patterns, meticulously categorized into **Creational**, **Structural**, and **Behavioral** groups. These were not arbitrary groupings; rather, they emerged from extensive real-world experience. Each pattern was documented with a consistent format, including **Intent**, **Motivation**, **Structure**, and **Consequences**, providing a template for discussing and applying these solutions.

Ongoing Development and Diversification

The original 23 patterns were never meant to be exhaustive. As software complexity and paradigms evolved—through distributed systems, agile methodologies, domain-driven design, and more—new patterns emerged, while old ones were refined. Various fields within computing began developing their own specialized patterns: for example, concurrency patterns, enterprise integration patterns, and microservices patterns.

Modern pattern usage also reflects a shift to multiple programming paradigms. While the GoF book focuses on object-oriented solutions, languages like JavaScript, Python, Swift, and functional languages such as Haskell can adopt or adapt these strategies. Some patterns translate nearly directly, while others require rethinking in the context of closures, higher-order functions, or prototypes.

Textual Timeline of Key Milestones

Below is a textual representation of major events in the evolution of design patterns:

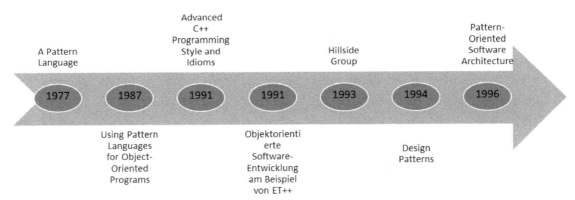

Figure 2: Major milestones tracing how design patterns originated, were formalized, and continue to evolve.

Lasting Impact on Software Industry

The influence of design patterns on modern software cannot be overstated. The patterns give teams a **common vocabulary**—reducing friction in design discussions, code reviews, and documentation. By encouraging **best practices** such as loose coupling, separation of concerns, and modular design, patterns help craft software that is both resilient and extensible.

Not only do design patterns enhance communication among developers, but they also bridge the gap between novices and experts. Junior developers, armed with pattern knowledge, can more easily decipher complex codebases if they recognize patterns already in use. Senior engineers can rely on patterns to standardize solutions across diverse teams and components, thus ensuring consistency in large-scale systems.

1.3 Importance of Design Patterns in Software Engineering

Why do design patterns matter so much? While we have hinted at several benefits—like reusability, communication, and maintainability—this section offers a deeper dive into the multifaceted advantages they bring to the table.

Key Differentiations	Software Architecture Patterns	Design Patterns
Scope	Software architecture is decided in the design phase.	Design Patterns are dealt with in the building phase.
Abstraction	Software architecture is like a blueprint - a high-level idea of the data flow, components, and interactions between them.	A more detailed design pattern focuses on solving specific design problems within a component.
Granularity	It provides a broad view of the system and addresses large-scale components and their interactions.	A design pattern addresses small-scale design issues within a component or a class.
Reusability	An architectural pattern can be reused across different projects with similar requirements.	It can be reused within the same project to solve recurring design problems.
Relationship	It defines the overall structure, and communication patterns, and organization of components.	It solves common design problems like object creation, interaction, and behavior.
Time of Application	An architectural pattern is implemented at a very early stage of the SDLC.	A design pattern is implemented during the coding phase of software development.
Examples	Layered Architecture, Client-Server Architecture, Microservices, MVC, etc.	Singleton, Factory Method, Observer, Strategy, etc.

Enhancing Code Reusability and Maintainability

One of the central purposes of design patterns is to **abstract reusable solutions** to recurring challenges. Instead of writing ad hoc code for every scenario, you adopt a tried-and-tested approach. This reusability extends beyond your specific project; it influences how future team members or even entirely separate teams might tackle similar problems.

Moreover, because design patterns are structured in a **well-documented** manner, maintaining and evolving the code is less error-prone. When you recognize that a specific area of the code is implemented using, say, the **Strategy Pattern,** you immediately know where to look if you need to add new algorithms or alter existing ones. This clarity shortens the onboarding curve for new developers and reduces the likelihood of introducing defects when making changes.

Example Scenario: Imagine a web application that needs to generate multiple variations of a report (PDF, Excel, and HTML). Implementing each type from scratch might lead to repetitive code. However, using a pattern like **Strategy** allows you to define a single interface for report generation while offering different concrete strategies for each format. This approach significantly reduces duplicate logic and positions you to add new report formats in the future with minimal disruption.

Facilitating Communication Among Developers

Software engineering is often a **collaborative** endeavor. Whether you are working with colleagues, open-source contributors, or clients, the ability to articulate design decisions succinctly is invaluable. By using pattern names, you can compress complex architectural ideas into a single term. A statement like "We'll use the **Observer Pattern** for the event system" communicates a clear direction instantly.

Moreover, code reviews become more efficient because both reviewer and author are speaking the same conceptual language. Rather than diving into a line-by-line explanation of how event observers are managed, the pattern reference signals to the reviewer what to expect, what to verify, and how to reason about expansions or modifications.

Promoting Best Practices and a Robust Architecture

Design patterns inherently encourage **principles of good design**. They embody practices like **loose coupling, encapsulation, information hiding,** and **single responsibility**—all pillars of robust architecture. By adopting design patterns in your workflow, you are essentially incorporating these principles into your project from the get-go.

When a codebase consistently employs patterns, the architecture often emerges in a **cleaner**, more modular form. This structural integrity translates into systems that are more **resilient** to change. New requirements or feature expansions can be introduced without causing a domino effect of breakages across the system.

Example: Dependency Injection and Testing: Consider how patterns that encourage

dependency injection automatically make your system more testable. By injecting dependencies rather than hard-coding them, you can easily swap out real implementations for mocks in a testing environment. Patterns such as the Factory Method or a Service Locator can reinforce this approach, making your code simpler to maintain and test in the long run.

Cost Reduction and Time Efficiency

Time is money in software development. Crafting a solution from scratch for each problem is expensive and tedious. Design patterns, by comparison, are **shortcuts** to robust solutions. Leveraging them can:

1. **Decrease Development Time:** Once a developer recognizes a relevant pattern, much of the architectural legwork is already done.
2. **Reduce Maintenance Costs:** Patterns lead to code that is easier to debug and extend. Fewer cycles are wasted on patching brittle code or re-engineering flawed modules.
3. **Accelerate Onboarding:** New team members who are familiar with common design patterns can quickly adapt to the established architecture, speeding up their ability to contribute.

Encouraging Scalability and Flexibility

Scalability is not only about handling more users or transactions. It is also about ensuring your system architecture can gracefully evolve. Patterns that encourage loose coupling and clear separation of concerns—such as the Observer or Mediator patterns—help your system scale by neatly compartmentalizing logic. If you need to spin off a microservice or replace an internal algorithm, patterns make those transitions smoother.

Below is a textual diagram summarizing these core benefits:

Adapter	Bridge	Observer
Convert the interface of a class to another interface that clients expect.	Decouple an abstraction from its implementation so that the two can vary independently.	Notify multiple objects when the state of another object changes.
interface, class, conversion	implementation, abstraction, decoupling, independent variation	multiple objects, state change, notification

Decorator	Builder	Factory
Add behavior to an object dynamically without affecting the behavior of other objects.	Simplify the creation of complex objects with many optional parameters.	Dynamically create objects based on input, configuration, or business rules.
object behavior, dynamic addition, no effect on other objects	complex objects, optional parameters, simplified creation	object creation, dynamic, input, configuration, business rules

Template Method	Command	Proxy
Define the skeleton of an algorithm in a base class and let subclasses override specific steps.	Encapsulate a request as an object and pass it to invokers to execute.	Control access to an object by creating a surrogate that handles the request.
algorithm, skeleton, base class, specific steps, subclass	encapsulation, request, object, invokers, execution	access control, surrogate, request handling
Iterator	**Facade**	Composite
Traverse elements of a collection without exposing its underlying implementation.	Provide a unified interface to a set of interfaces in a subsystem to simplify their usage.	Compose objects into a tree structure to represent part-whole hierarchies.
collection, element traversal, implementation hiding	simplified usage, subsystem, interface, unification	tree structure, part-whole hierarchy, object composition
Flyweight	**Visitor**	**State**
Share objects to support large numbers of fine-grained objects efficiently.	Separate the algorithm from the object structure it operates on.	Alter an object's behavior when its state changes.
object sharing, fine-grained objects, efficiency	algorithm separation, object structure, operation	State change, notification

Figure 3: Overview of the primary reasons design patterns are vital in modern software engineering.

1.4 Types of Design Patterns

While the Gang of Four text remains the canonical reference for the original 23 patterns, patterns have proliferated far beyond that foundational set. Nonetheless, most patterns still fall under broad categorization that helps structure your thinking about when and how to apply them.

Creational Patterns

Creational patterns deal with **object construction mechanisms**, trying to create objects in a manner that suits the context. Their goal is to encapsulate knowledge about **which** concrete classes the system uses, and **how** to build or combine them.

- **Key Objective:** Separate the client from the process of actual creation, thus reducing dependencies and coupling.
- **Examples (to be covered in later chapters):** Singleton, Factory Method, Abstract Factory, Builder, Prototype.

Structural Patterns

Structural patterns revolve around **class and object composition**, ensuring that if one part of the system changes, the overall structure remains relatively stable. These patterns often help you form larger structures or simplify relationships between components.

- Key Objective: Optimize the structure of classes and objects to ensure flexibility and efficiency in how parts interrelate.
- Examples (to be covered in later chapters): Adapter, Bridge, Composite, Decorator, Facade, Flyweight, Proxy.

Behavioral Patterns

Behavioral patterns outline the interaction and responsibility distribution among objects. Their purpose is to simplify how objects communicate or manage the flow of control in a system, ensuring interactions are clear, consistent, and maintainable.

- **Key Objective:** Define communication patterns and assignment of responsibilities among objects to improve flexibility and clarity.
- **Examples (to be covered in later chapters):** Chain of Responsibility, Command, Interpreter, Iterator, Mediator, Memento, Observer, State, Strategy, Template Method, Visitor.

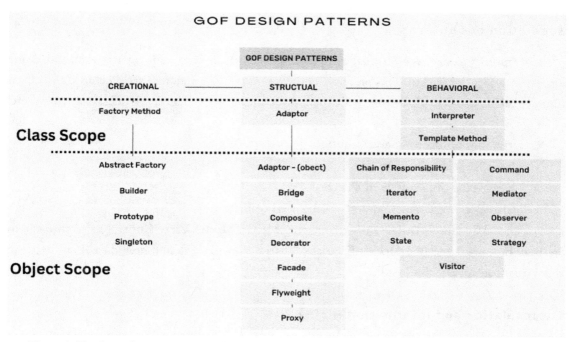

Figure 4: Traditional categorization of design patterns into creational, structural, and behavioral groups.

Beyond the GoF Patterns

Over the years, many other patterns have emerged, such as **Model-View-Controller (MVC)** for GUIs and web applications, **Repository** and **Service** patterns for domain-driven design, and even specialized patterns for **microservices** (like **Circuit Breaker** or **Saga**). While these might be covered in specialized or advanced chapters, understanding the fundamental taxonomy (creational, structural, behavioral) provides an excellent starting point to map out how different solutions fit into the broader software design landscape.

Practical Implications of Classification

Why do we categorize design patterns? These categories help you **quickly zero** in on potential solutions. If your issue involves controlling how objects are instantiated, you look at the **Creational** category; if it's about arranging classes for better maintainability, consider **Structural**. This classification is also a roadmap for deeper study, ensuring that patterns are not learned in an ad hoc manner but within a conceptual framework that highlights similarities and differences.

1.5 Design Principles Behind Patterns

Design patterns are not conjured out of thin air. They are often the natural extension of fundamental principles that guide what "good" software design looks like. Being aware of these principles helps you understand why patterns work and when they might be the right fit.

Separation of Concerns

Separation of Concerns states that a program should be split into distinct parts, each addressing a specific aspect or concern. This principle underlies most well-structured architectures. Instead of lumping all logic into one place, separate them: user interface logic, business rules, data access, etc.

Patterns that enforce separation often:
- Improve maintainability.
- Reduce the ripple effect of changes.
- Clarify responsibilities among various parts of the system.

For example, many frameworks adopt the **MVC (Model-View-Controller)** approach to separate business logic (the Model) from the UI (the View) and define how data flows between them (the Controller).

Encapsulation and Information Hiding

Encapsulation ensures internal details of a component (class, module, microservice) remain hidden behind a **well-defined interface**. Patterns like **Facade** or **Factory** leverage encapsulation to hide complexities. When a complex subsystem or object construction logic is wrapped inside a simpler interface, it **lowers cognitive load** for the client.
- **Advantages:**
  - Reduced interdependencies among classes.
  - Ease of swapping implementations without breaking dependent code.

Modularity and Reusability

A system is modular if it is decomposed into independent, cohesive units that can be developed, maintained, and tested in isolation. Design patterns often promote reusability by providing standard ways to attach, remove, or combine modules. For instance, the Decorator Pattern allows you to wrap objects with additional behavior dynamically, facilitating code reuse without duplication.

The SOLID Principles

Among the most celebrated sets of design guidelines are the SOLID principles, which you can see implemented or facilitated by many design patterns:

1. **Single Responsibility Principle (SRP):** A class should have a single responsibility. Patterns that funnel related behavior into one place—like State for encapsulating an object's state transitions—reinforce SRP.

2. **Open/Closed Principle (OCP):** Software entities should be open for extension, but closed for modification. Patterns such as Strategy or Template Method let you add new behavior or implementations with minimal alteration to the existing code.

3. **Liskov Substitution Principle (LSP):** Subtypes must be replaceable for their base types without breaking functionality. Patterns that rely on polymorphism—like Factory Method or Bridge—often embody LSP by ensuring derived classes behave consistently.

4. **Interface Segregation Principle (ISP):** Clients should not be forced to depend on interfaces they do not use. Patterns encouraging multiple small, specialized interfaces (rather than a single "god" interface) reflect ISP.

5. **Dependency Inversion Principle (DIP):** Depend on abstractions, not concretions. Many patterns revolve around the notion of inverting dependencies—whether in the form of injecting dependencies at runtime or referencing abstract interfaces rather than concrete classes.

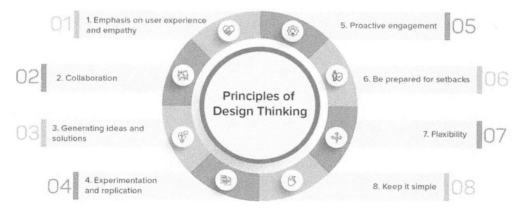

Figure 5: Visual overview of key design principles that form the backbone of many design patterns.

Why Principles Matter

Without these principles, design patterns might be applied in a superficial manner—leading to code that merely uses the structure of a pattern without reaping its actual benefits. When you combine robust principles with practical patterns, your software design becomes far more than the sum of its parts. This synergy is why seasoned developers stress learning not just the "how" but the "why" of patterns.

Conclusion

The study and application of design patterns is a journey that enriches every stage of the software development life cycle, from initial design and implementation to testing and maintenance. Mastering them grants you both technical depth and a shared language that resonates across teams, companies, and industries.

As you move forward to subsequent chapters, keep this foundational chapter in mind. You now have the conceptual lenses (and vocabulary) to identify, understand, and adapt patterns to your unique software challenges. The upcoming chapters will delve into specific pattern families—Creational, Structural, and Behavioral—providing detailed examples, best practices, and advanced use cases. By the time you finish this book, you'll be fluent in the language of patterns and prepared to craft robust, elegant solutions for even the most intricate of software systems.

Chapter 2: Creational Design Patterns

Creating objects in software may sound straightforward—just call a constructor, right? In practice, the details of object creation can have significant ramifications for the flexibility, maintainability, and performance of an entire system. **Creational Design Patterns** address these challenges by offering time-tested approaches that separate object creation from the rest of the application logic. This chapter thoroughly explores the major creational patterns, illustrating how they can streamline your design process and reduce coupling between classes.

2.1 Understanding Creational Patterns

Creational patterns are specifically about **controlling how objects are constructed**. Rather than letting client code call constructors directly, creational patterns encapsulate the creation logic in specialized objects or methods. The result is that client code remains agnostic to *which* concrete classes are instantiated or *how* they are created. This promotes loose coupling, a hallmark of well-designed systems.

Why We Need Creational Patterns

1. **Complexity of Object Construction:** Certain objects have intricate initialization sequences. For instance, you might need to ensure dependencies are injected, configurations are loaded, or data is validated. Offloading this complexity to a pattern like **Builder** keeps client code clean and easier to read.
2. **Avoiding Repetition and Duplication:** If multiple parts of a system need similar objects, creation logic can become repetitive. Creational patterns like **Factory Method** or **Abstract Factory** let you centralize and streamline these procedures, reducing code duplication.
3. **Controlling Object Lifecycles:** Sometimes you need exact control over the number or lifecycle of objects. The **Singleton** pattern enforces that only one instance of a class can

exist at a time, which can be critical for certain resources (e.g., global logging facilities).

4. **Decoupling Clients from Concrete Implementations:** Client code often does not need to know the specific classes of objects—it only cares about the interface or abstract type. Patterns that **abstract away** the instantiation details (like **Factory Method**) allow you to swap out implementations with minimal disruption.

Common Features Across Creational Patterns

Although each creational pattern has unique structural elements, they share certain philosophies:

- **Encapsulation of Creation Logic:** Making object creation a first-class concern, often hidden behind an interface or base class.
- **Flexibility and Extensibility:** By localizing object-creation responsibilities, changes in how objects are created (or which objects are created) have minimal impact on other parts of the system.
- **Reduced Coupling:** Client code remains blissfully unaware of the complexities beneath the surface, focusing on higher-level tasks rather than the specifics of building objects.

2.2 Singleton Pattern

The **Singleton** pattern is often the first encountered by developers, primarily because it addresses a straightforward requirement: ensuring only one instance of a particular class exists in the entire application. While straightforward in concept, there are subtle nuances—particularly regarding concurrency, performance, and testing—that merit deeper exploration.

2.2.1 Context and Motivation

Some resources or services within an application need to be accessed globally, but you only want (or can only afford) *one* instance. Typical examples include:

- A **logging facility** that captures system-wide events.
- A **configuration manager** that loads settings from environment variables or external files.
- A **database connection pool** (though in practice, a pool might have multiple connections internally, the manager often acts like a single coordinator).

If you let any part of the code create new instances of these classes at will, you risk duplication of resources, inconsistent state, or performance bottlenecks from re-initializing complex objects multiple times.

2.2.2 Structure and Participants

- **Singleton Class:** Holds a reference to the sole instance and usually exposes a static getter method (e.g., getInstance() or similar). The constructor is made **private** or **protected**, preventing external instantiation.

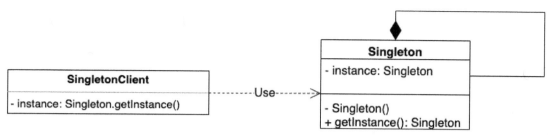

2.2.3 Implementation Details

1. **Private Constructor:** Ensures code outside the class cannot create additional objects.
2. **Static Getter:** A getInstance() method returns the instance, creating it upon the first request if it does not already exist.
3. **Thread Safety (if needed):** In multi-threaded contexts, the creation and return of the single instance must be synchronized to avoid race conditions. Double-checked locking, eager initialization, or other strategies may be employed.
4. **Lazy vs. Eager Initialization:**
   - **Lazy:** The instance is created only when needed.
   - **Eager:** The instance is created when the class is loaded. This can be faster for repeated calls but might waste resources if the singleton is never used.

Example (Pseudo-Code)

```
class GlobalLogger {
    private static GlobalLogger instance;
    private List<String> logEntries;

    // Private constructor prevents direct instantiation
    private GlobalLogger() {
        logEntries = new ArrayList<String>();
    }

    public static synchronized GlobalLogger getInstance() {
        if (instance == null) {
            instance = new GlobalLogger();
        }
        return instance;
    }

    public void log(String message) {
```

```
        logEntries.add(message);
    }

    public List<String> getLogEntries() {
        return Collections.unmodifiableList(logEntries);
    }
}
```

Note: Thread-safe approaches can vary by language. In some languages, static initialization blocks or other concurrency constructs can reduce overhead.

2.2.4 Advantages and Disadvantages

- **Advantages**:
  - o Guaranteed single instance.
  - o Straightforward global access.
  - o Can preserve state across the entire application run.
- **Disadvantages**:
  - o Difficult to unit test (mocks or multiple instances can be tricky).
  - o Global state can lead to hidden dependencies, making code less clear.
  - o In multi-threaded applications, synchronization must be handled carefully.

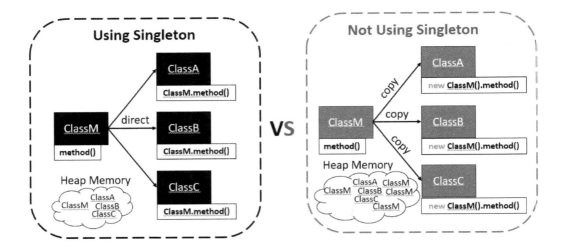

2.2.5 Real-World Examples

- **Java's Runtime class**: The Runtime.getRuntime() method is a de-facto Singleton giving you environment-level operations (like executing external processes).
- **Game engines**: Sometimes enforce a single "GameWorld" or "RenderingManager" instance to coordinate shared resources.

2.3 Factory Method Pattern

Factory Method addresses the scenario in which a superclass or interface defines a method for object creation, but *subclasses* decide which specific class to instantiate. This fosters loose coupling by deferring the choice of concrete classes to the subclasses or implementing classes.

2.3.1 Context and Motivation

Often, you have a class that relies on objects conforming to a particular interface but *doesn't* need to know *which* concrete implementation it's working with. For instance, you might want to build different types of dialog boxes—desktop vs. web forms—using the same code. The Factory Method can produce the concrete implementations of these dialog objects without polluting higher-level code with if-else or switch statements.

2.3.2 Structure and Participants

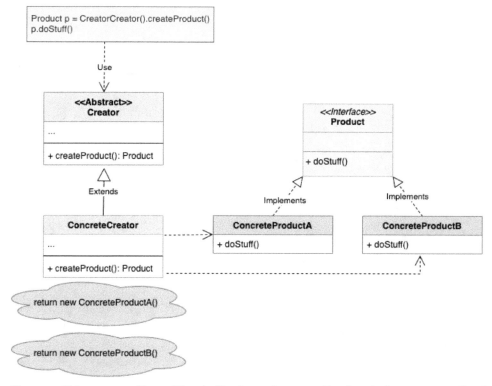

1. **Creator (Abstract or Base Class):** Declares the createProduct() that returns a Product.
2. **ConcreteCreator:** Implements createProduct() to produce a specific type of Product.
3. **Product (Interface or Abstract Class):** Defines the general contract for objects returned by the factory.
4. **ConcreteProduct:** Different implementations of the Product interface, each tailored to specific needs.

25

2.3.3 Implementation Details

- **Factory Method vs. Constructor:** Instead of calling new ProductA(), client code calls createProduct(), which in turn creates the product.
- **Override in Subclasses:** The "creator" class might be abstract, forcing subclasses to override createProduct(). Alternatively, the creator can be concrete but delegates decisions to a protected method that subclasses override if desired.

Example (Pseudo-Code)

Imagine an application that can generate either PDF documents or HTML documents:

```
abstract class DocumentCreator {
    // The "Factory Method"
    protected abstract Document createDocument();

    public void renderDocument() {
        Document doc = createDocument();
        doc.render();
    }
}


class PDFDocumentCreator extends DocumentCreator {
    @Override
    protected Document createDocument() {
        return new PDFDocument();
    }
}


class HTMLDocumentCreator extends DocumentCreator {
    @Override
    protected Document createDocument() {
        return new HTMLDocument();
    }
}


// Product interface
interface Document {
    void render();
}
```

```
// Concrete Products
class PDFDocument implements Document {
  @Override
  public void render() {
    System.out.println("Rendering PDF...");
  }
}

class HTMLDocument implements Document {
  @Override
  public void render() {
    System.out.println("Rendering HTML...");
  }
}
```

2.3.4 Advantages and Disadvantages

- **Advantages**:
  - o Flexibility: Extend the hierarchy with new ConcreteProduct classes without touching existing code.
  - o Single Responsibility: The creation logic is localized to specific subclasses.
  - o Avoids monolithic "if-else" or "switch" statements in one big factory.
- **Disadvantages**:
  - o Can lead to a proliferation of subclasses if your system has many product variants.
  - o Sometimes overkill if you only need straightforward object creation.

2.3.5 Real-World Examples

- **Dialog Boxes in GUI Frameworks**: Different OS or frameworks might require different rendering logic, but the high-level workflow remains the same.
- **Parsing Libraries**: A base parser might define createToken(), but specialized languages override it to return different token types.

2.4 Abstract Factory Pattern

Where the Factory Method focuses on creating *one* product type, **Abstract Factory** coordinates the creation of related objects (often from multiple product families). This pattern is particularly handy when a subsystem needs to support multiple "themes" or "platforms," each with its own consistent set of product variants.

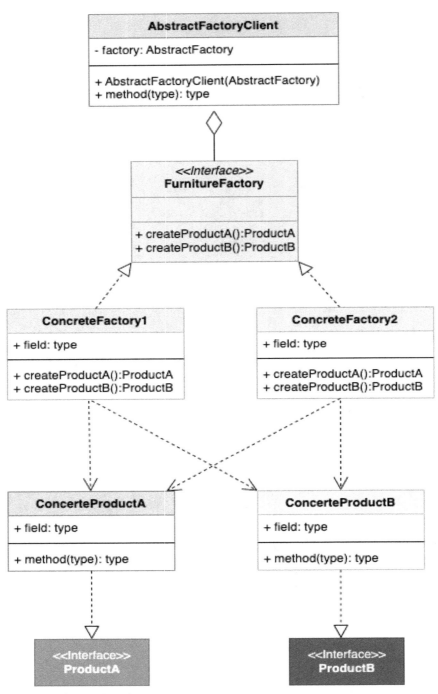

2.4.1 Context and Motivation

Suppose you are building a cross-platform UI toolkit that must generate interface elements for Windows, Linux, and macOS. Each platform has different look-and-feel widgets (like buttons, scroll bars, or text inputs). Instead of scattering if-else checks for each platform in your code, you can define an **Abstract Factory** that produces the entire family of UI widgets for a specific platform. By switching which concrete factory you use, you change the entire UI "theme" seamlessly.

2.4.2 Structure and Participants

1. **AbstractFactory**: Declares methods for creating each product in the family (e.g., button, text field, etc.).
2. **ConcreteFactory**: Implements methods to create products of a particular variant (e.g., Windows or macOS).
3. **AbstractProduct**: Declares the interface for a type of product (e.g., Button).
4. **ConcreteProduct**: Implementation that belongs to one product family (e.g., ProductA or ProductB).

2.4.3 Implementation Details

- **Organizing the Families**: Each concrete factory is responsible for the entire set of product variants.
- **Ensuring Consistency**: A single factory invocation can create multiple interdependent objects. This ensures they are compatible or aesthetically consistent.
- **Adding New Products**: If you introduce a new kind of product to each family (for instance, a Slider), you update the abstract factory interface and each concrete factory accordingly.

Example (Pseudo-Code)

```
// Abstract Factory
interface GUIFactory {
    Button createButton();
    TextField createTextField();
}


// Concrete Factories
class WinFactory implements GUIFactory {
    public Button createButton() {
        return new WinButton();
    }
    public TextField createTextField() {
        return new WinTextField();
```

```java
    }
}

class MacFactory implements GUIFactory {
    public Button createButton() {
        return new MacButton();
    }
    public TextField createTextField() {
        return new MacTextField();
    }
}

// Abstract Product interfaces
interface Button {
    void click();
}

interface TextField {
    void setText(String text);
}

// Concrete Products
class WinButton implements Button {
    public void click() {
        System.out.println("Windows-style button clicked");
    }
}

class WinTextField implements TextField {
    public void setText(String text) {
        System.out.println("Windows text field set: " + text);
    }
}

class MacButton implements Button {
    public void click() {
        System.out.println("macOS-style button clicked");
    }
}
```

```
class MacTextField implements TextField {
  public void setText(String text) {
    System.out.println("macOS text field set: " + text);
  }
}

// Client code
class Application {
  private GUIFactory guiFactory;
  private Button button;
  private TextField textField;

  public Application(GUIFactory factory) {
    this.guiFactory = factory;
    this.button = guiFactory.createButton();
    this.textField = guiFactory.createTextField();
  }

  public void run() {
    button.click();
    textField.setText("Hello Abstract Factory!");
  }
}
```

2.4.4 Advantages and Disadvantages

- **Advantages**:
  - o Ensures product families remain compatible.
  - o Centralizes creation of related objects, maintaining a consistent theme or platform logic.
  - o Isolates clients from concrete classes.
- **Disadvantages**:
  - o Extending a product family often requires modifying the abstract factory interface (and all its concrete implementations).
  - o Can introduce complexity if you only need to create one product type.

2.4.5 Real-World Examples

- **Cross-Platform GUI Libraries** such as Qt or Java's AWT/Swing employ the principle of abstract factories to manage differences among OS.
- **Game Development**: Different "skins" or "themes" for in-game objects (medieval vs. sci-

fi) might be produced via an abstract factory.

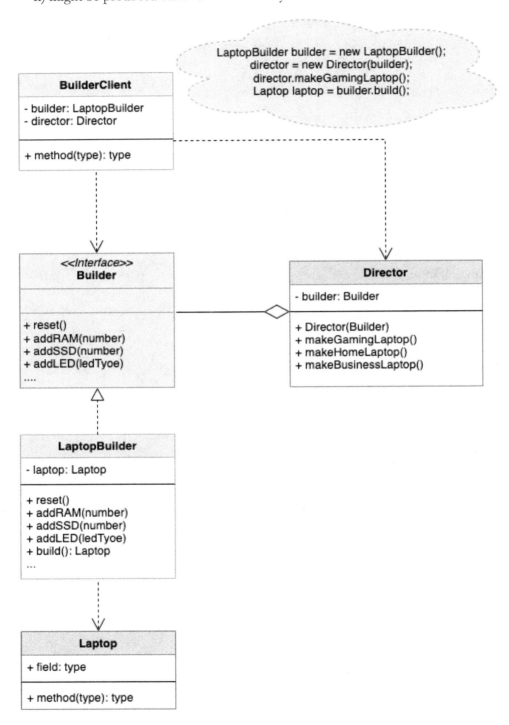

2.5 Builder Pattern

Sometimes objects have complicated initialization sequences that go beyond a simple constructor. The **Builder** pattern separates object construction (the "how") from the final representation (the "what"), offering a step-by-step approach. This approach is especially handy when an object has many optional attributes or sub-objects.

2.5.1 Context and Motivation

Consider a scenario where you're constructing a **complex object** with multiple nested fields or hierarchical data, such as:

- Assembling a **house** object with rooms, doors, windows, a garage, a backyard, etc.
- Creating a **meal** with multiple courses, each having sub-parts (appetizers, drinks, main courses, desserts).
- Generating a **document** that includes headers, footers, sections, indexes, etc.

If you try to funnel all these configurations into a single constructor with a dozen parameters, it becomes unwieldy and error-prone. Builder allows you to create this object step-by-step, with each step focusing on a particular aspect or component.

2.5.2 Structure and Participants

1. **Builder**: Declares a set of methods for creating different parts of the product.
2. **ConcreteBuilder**: Implements these methods to assemble a specific representation of the product. Stores the final product inside.
3. **Director**: Oversees the building process, calling builder methods in a particular sequence.
4. **Product (ComplexObj)**: The complex object being assembled.

2.5.3 Implementation Details

- **Optional Director**: Using a Director is common but optional. Sometimes the client code directly calls Builder methods in whichever order is desired.
- **Fluent Interface**: Many builder implementations use a fluent style, returning the this reference from each builder method to allow method chaining.
- **Reusability**: You can reuse the same ConcreteBuilder to build multiple products if you reset its state properly.

Example (Pseudo-Code)

Let's look at a simplified example of building a **Meal** with a main course, a side, and a drink:

```
// Product
class Meal {
    private String mainCourse;
    private String side;
    private String drink;
```

```java
    // getters and setters omitted for brevity
}

// Builder interface
interface MealBuilder {
    void buildMainCourse(String main);
    void buildSide(String side);
    void buildDrink(String drink);
    Meal getMeal();
}

// Concrete Builder
class StandardMealBuilder implements MealBuilder {
    private Meal meal;

    public StandardMealBuilder() {
        meal = new Meal();
    }

    @Override
    public void buildMainCourse(String main) {
        meal.setMainCourse(main);
    }

    @Override
    public void buildSide(String side) {
        meal.setSide(side);
    }

    @Override
    public void buildDrink(String drink) {
        meal.setDrink(drink);
    }

    @Override
    public Meal getMeal() {
        return meal;
    }
}
```

```
// Director
class MealDirector {
   public Meal makeStandardMeal(MealBuilder builder) {
      builder.buildMainCourse("Hamburger");
      builder.buildSide("Fries");
      builder.buildDrink("Cola");
      return builder.getMeal();
   }

   public Meal makeVegetarianMeal(MealBuilder builder) {
      builder.buildMainCourse("Veggie Burger");
      builder.buildSide("Salad");
      builder.buildDrink("Juice");
      return builder.getMeal();
   }
}

// Client usage
class Restaurant {
   public void serveMeals() {
      MealDirector director = new MealDirector();
      MealBuilder builder = new StandardMealBuilder();

      Meal standard = director.makeStandardMeal(builder);
      Meal vegetarian = director.makeVegetarianMeal(builder);
   }
}
```

2.5.4 Advantages and Disadvantages

- **Advantages**:
    - Clarifies complex object construction.
    - Enables stepwise (and optional) initialization.
    - Promotes immutability if used properly (by returning a built object).
- **Disadvantages**:
    - Overkill for simpler objects.
    - Requires more classes (Builder, Director) and thus more boilerplate.

2.5.5 Real-World Examples

- **String Builders** in various programming languages that construct complex strings or large text blocks step by step.
- **ORM (Object-Relational Mapping)** frameworks sometimes use builder-like patterns to assemble queries or entities with multiple relationships.

2.6 Prototype Pattern

In some scenarios, creating new objects by copying (or "cloning") an existing prototype can be more efficient or more straightforward than building from scratch. The **Prototype** pattern allows you to create new objects by duplicating existing ones, effectively "stamping out" instances with pre-initialized values.

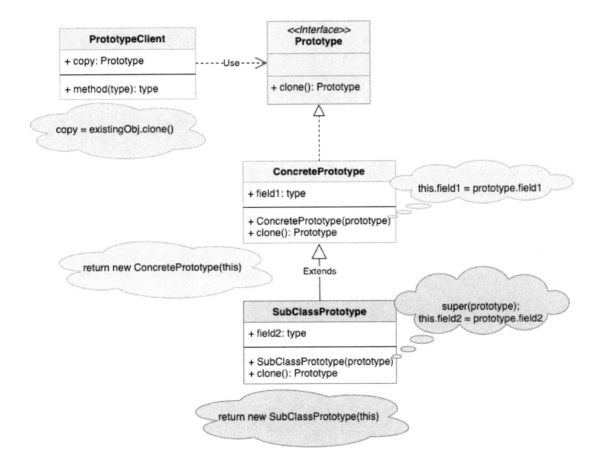

2.6.1 Context and Motivation

Consider applications where object creation is expensive, either computationally or in terms of resource usage. Creating a new instance from scratch might involve reading from a database, performing expensive calculations, or retrieving large data sets. If you already have an object with these states or settings prepared, cloning it can be faster and simpler.

36

Another context is when a system dynamically loads classes or object configurations at runtime. Instead of hardcoding how objects are instantiated, the system can store prototypes of objects, which can then be cloned on demand.

2.6.2 Structure and Participants

(Clients hold references to prototypes and invoke clone() to get new instances)
1. **Prototype**: Declares a clone() method for duplicating itself.
2. **ConcretePrototype**: Implements the clone() method, copying relevant fields to produce a new object.
3. **Client**: Maintains references to a set of prototypes from which it clones objects.

2.6.3 Implementation Details

- **Shallow vs. Deep Copy**: A shallow copy duplicates the top-level object, but references to nested objects remain the same. A deep copy creates entirely new copies of nested objects, too.
- **Registration of Prototypes**: Typically, you store prototypes in a registry (a hash map or dictionary) keyed by some identifier. Clients retrieve the desired prototype and call clone().
- **Customization after Cloning**: Often, after you clone a prototype, you tweak a few properties to tailor it to a specific usage.

Example (Pseudo-Code)

```
interface Shape extends Cloneable {
    Shape clone();
    void draw();
}


class Rectangle implements Shape {
    private int width;
    private int height;

    public Rectangle(int w, int h) {
        width = w;
        height = h;
    }

    @Override
    public Shape clone() {
        // Shallow copy example (primitive fields only)
        return new Rectangle(this.width, this.height);
```

```java
  }

  @Override
  public void draw() {
    System.out.println("Drawing rectangle: " + width + "x" + height);
  }
}

class ShapeRegistry {
  private Map<String, Shape> prototypes = new HashMap<>();

  public void addPrototype(String key, Shape shape) {
    prototypes.put(key, shape);
  }

  public Shape getPrototype(String key) {
    Shape prototype = prototypes.get(key);
    if (prototype != null) {
      return prototype.clone();
    }
    return null;
  }
}

// Usage
class DrawingApp {
  public static void main(String[] args) {
    ShapeRegistry registry = new ShapeRegistry();
    registry.addPrototype("big-rect", new Rectangle(100, 50));

    Shape shape1 = registry.getPrototype("big-rect");
    shape1.draw(); // "Drawing rectangle: 100x50"

    // We could clone again
    Shape shape2 = registry.getPrototype("big-rect");
    shape2.draw(); // "Drawing rectangle: 100x50"
  }
}
```

- **Advantages**:
  - ○ Useful for dynamic or runtime-based object creation.
  - ○ Can drastically reduce the cost of repeatedly constructing complex objects.
  - ○ Avoids coupling to concrete classes if you manage prototypes via an interface.
- **Disadvantages**:
  - ○ Requires implementing clone logic carefully, especially for deep copies.
  - ○ Potential for confusion if your system is heavily reliant on references and shared data.
  - ○ Overlapping responsibilities if you already have a robust factory system in place.

2.6.5 Real-World Examples

- **GUI Editors** often let users clone (duplicate) shapes or components with a single click rather than building them anew.

- **Game Items**: Many game engines store prototypes of enemy or item types, and when they need a new instance, they simply clone an existing prototype.

2.7 Comparing Creational Patterns

Now that we have covered the five major Creational Patterns—**Singleton, Factory Method, Abstract Factory, Builder, and Prototype**—it is instructive to compare and contrast them to clarify their use cases and potential overlaps.

2.7.1 High-Level Distinctions

1. **Singleton**: Focuses on restricting instantiation to exactly one object and providing a global point of access.
2. **Factory Method**: A method within a class that decides which concrete product subclass gets created.
3. **Abstract Factory**: Bundles the creation of multiple, related product types under a consistent interface.
4. **Builder**: Separates the construction process of a complex object from its representation, enabling stepwise assembly.
5. **Prototype**: Creates objects by cloning existing instances.

2.7.2 When to Use Each Pattern

Pattern	Use When...
Singleton	You must have exactly one instance of a class, typically globally accessed.
Factory Method	You want subclasses or other classes to decide which concrete product to instantiate, but focus on a single product type at a time.
Abstract Factory	You need to create families of related objects without hardcoding their classes.
Builder	You have a complex object with multiple optional components or stepwise creation sequences.
Prototype	You want to create new objects by copying or "stamping out" existing pre-configured prototypes.

2.7.3 Potential Overlaps

- **Factory Method vs. Abstract Factory**: Abstract Factory can be seen as a collection of factory methods grouped under one overarching interface.
- **Builder vs. Factory**: If your object has a simpler creation process (just picking a class), a factory pattern may suffice. If your object requires stepwise, customizable creation with numerous optional parts, Builder is preferable.
- **Prototype vs. Builders/Factories**: Instead of constructing each instance from scratch, Prototype reuses existing instance states. If you rarely need to replicate existing objects, Prototype might be less relevant.

2.8 Real-World Scenarios for Creational Patterns

While each pattern's discussion included examples, it can be illuminating to see how multiple creational patterns might interact in complex real-world systems. This section offers a broader perspective.

2.8.1 Complex UI Framework

- **Abstract Factory**: Chooses an entire set of widgets depending on the platform or skin.
- **Builder**: Constructs composite UI elements (like forms or wizards) step by step, ensuring each part is properly initialized.
- **Singleton**: Manages a single configuration manager or theme manager for the entire UI framework.

2.8.2 Level Editing Tool in Game Development

- **Prototype**: The tool keeps a library of "enemy prototypes," "environment object prototypes," etc., letting designers quickly clone them into new scenes.
- **Factory Method**: Each "theme" or "level type" might have a specialized factory for spawning region-specific or theme-specific items.
- **Singleton**: Possibly a single global manager for logging or resource caching.

2.8.3 Enterprise E-Commerce Platform

- **Abstract Factory**: Creating "Checkout Components" for different countries or currencies (cart, tax calculator, shipping module).
- **Builder**: Generating complex "Order" objects that gather data from many sources (user info, payment gateway, promotions).
- **Prototype**: Possibly reusing default configurations for typical product listings or discount strategies.

2.9 Common Pitfalls & Best Practices

Creational patterns can greatly simplify your design, but they are not without their pitfalls. Awareness of these pitfalls ensures you implement these patterns effectively.

1. **Overusing Singleton**:
   - **Pitfall**: Singleton can become a **global variable in disguise**, leading to hidden dependencies and testing difficulties.
   - **Best Practice**: Use only if truly necessary. Alternatively, consider dependency injection frameworks, which can manage lifecycles of objects more gracefully.
2. **Proliferation of Factory Subclasses**:
   - **Pitfall**: For large systems, the **Factory Method** or **Abstract Factory** may lead to many small classes if each product variant is specialized.
   - **Best Practice**: Keep your product hierarchy organized. If creation logic is minor, consider a simpler approach (e.g., static creation methods).
3. **Misapplication of Builder**:
   - **Pitfall**: Using the **Builder** pattern for objects that have only one or two parameters can be overkill, adding unnecessary complexity.
   - **Best Practice**: Reserve it for objects that have multiple optional fields, complex assembly sequences, or require intermediate states.
4. **Managing Cloning Complexity in Prototype**:
   - **Pitfall**: Shallow copying might inadvertently cause multiple references to the same nested objects, leading to bugs. Deep copying can be costly and complicated.
   - **Best Practice**: Decide carefully which fields should be deep-copied vs. shallow-copied. Make sure to test thoroughly for side-effects.

5. **Unclear Product Interfaces in Abstract Factory:**
    o **Pitfall:** If the methods in your abstract factory or the product interfaces are not well-defined, you might end up with confusion about how objects relate.
    o **Best Practice:** Clearly define the roles and interactions of each product. Keep product families as cohesive sets.

Chapter 3: Structural Design Patterns

As software systems grow in size and complexity, the way in which **classes and objects** are **organized** becomes paramount. Even with robust creation practices (the subject of creational patterns), poorly structured systems can become brittle, unmanageable, or prone to duplication of code and functionality. **Structural design patterns** aim to solve these organizational challenges, focusing on the composition and relationships of classes and objects in ways that foster flexibility, modularity, and clarity.

Unlike creational patterns, which focus on *how* to instantiate objects, structural patterns concern themselves with *how* objects and classes collaborate, extend, or wrap one another to fulfill specific roles in a system. They frequently rely on concepts such as **inheritance** (class-based patterns), **interfaces**, and **aggregation or composition** (object-based patterns). By abstracting or encapsulating complexities behind simpler interfaces, structural patterns minimize the interdependencies that can otherwise bog down large codebases.

3.1 Overview of Structural Patterns

Before diving into individual patterns, it is worth summarizing the goals that structural patterns typically address. Many design issues stem from code that lacks a coherent structure:

- **Rigid Hierarchies**: Classes that inherit from one another in ways that lock in certain behaviors, making changes or additions risky.
- **Unclear Interfaces**: Multiple classes might overlap in roles, or legacy code may provide interfaces that are incompatible with new frameworks.
- **Duplicated Logic**: Without careful composition, the same logic can appear in multiple places.
- **Excessive Complexity**: Clients interacting with a large subsystem may have to understand every detail, leading to steep learning curves and tight coupling.

Structural patterns respond to these problems by offering **encapsulation**, **interface abstraction**, **component reuse**, and **tree-like or layered** organization. By systematically applying these patterns, architects and developers can maintain clarity and consistency even as projects expand.

3.2 Adapter Pattern

When two components need to work together but are at odds due to incompatible interfaces, an **Adapter** (also sometimes referred to as a **Wrapper**) can reconcile these differences. This pattern allows existing classes to function under a new interface, removing the need to rewrite or deeply integrate them.

3.2.1 Context and Motivation

Developers frequently need to integrate with **legacy code**, external libraries, or third-party services that do not match the interfaces or naming conventions used in the new or existing system. Rather than modifying the existing code, which might be impossible or impractical, the Adapter pattern provides a way to "translate" between the "client's" expected interface and the "adaptee's" actual interface.

For instance, in a software tool that displays shapes, you might have a new interface Shape2D with methods like draw() and resize(). However, you also need to incorporate an older or third-party library that represents shapes differently, perhaps with methods like display(int x, int y, int width, int height). An adapter can implement Shape2D but internally delegate to the existing library calls, bridging the mismatch.

3.2.2 Structure and Participants

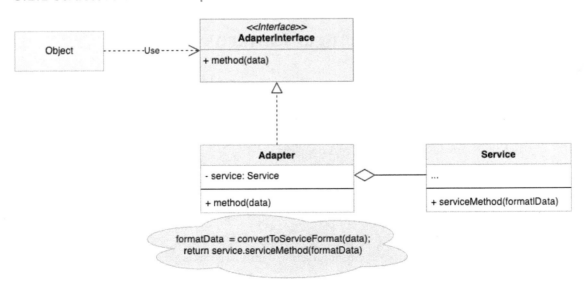

1. **Target**: The interface expected by the client.
2. **Adapter**: Implements the Target interface and holds a reference to an Adaptee object. Translates calls from the Target interface to the Adaptee's methods.
3. **Adaptee**: The existing or incompatible class that needs to be used by the client.

3.2.3 Implementation Details

- **Class Adapter vs. Object Adapter**:
  - **Class adapter** (multiple inheritance, possible in languages like C++): The adapter inherits from both the Target interface and the Adaptee class.
  - **Object adapter** (more common in languages without multiple inheritance): The adapter implements the Target interface and **has-a** Adaptee instance internally.
- **Method Translation**: The adapter's methods typically do some parameter transformation or re-mapping before calling the Adaptee's methods.
- **State Management**: The adapter may need to maintain internal state to coordinate data between the client's perspective and the adaptee's.

Example (Pseudo-Code)

```
// Target interface
interface Shape2D {
    void draw(int x, int y, int width, int height);
    void resize(double scale);
}


// Adaptee: existing library
class LegacyRectangle {
    public void display(int x1, int y1, int x2, int y2) {
        System.out.println("Legacy rectangle from (" + x1 + ", " + y1
                + ") to (" + x2 + ", " + y2 + ")");
    }
}


// Adapter
class RectangleAdapter implements Shape2D {
    private LegacyRectangle adaptee;
    private int x, y, width, height;

    public RectangleAdapter(LegacyRectangle legacyRect) {
        this.adaptee = legacyRect;
```

```
    }

    @Override
    public void draw(int x, int y, int width, int height) {
        this.x = x;
        this.y = y;
        this.width = width;
        this.height = height;
        // Convert (x, y, width, height) to (x1, y1, x2, y2)
        adaptee.display(x, y, x + width, y + height);
    }

    @Override
    public void resize(double scale) {
        this.width *= scale;
        this.height *= scale;
        adaptee.display(x, y, x + width, y + height);
    }
}
```

3.2.4 Advantages and Disadvantages

- **Advantages**:
    - o Allows integration with otherwise incompatible code or libraries.
    - o Doesn't require modifying the Adaptee, preserving its integrity.
    - o Enables existing classes to be reused in new contexts.
- **Disadvantages**:
    - o Adds an extra layer of indirection, potentially complicating debugging.
    - o The adapter might become complex if the interfaces differ significantly.

3.2.5 Real-World Examples

- **Software Wrappers** for cross-compatibility with different OS-level APIs.
- **Payment Gateways**: Adapters can unify multiple third-party payment providers (PayPal, Stripe, etc.) behind a single internal interface.
- **Data Format Adapters**: Transforming JSON-based services into a system expecting XML inputs, or vice versa.

3.3 Bridge Pattern

While Adapter focuses on reconciling incompatible interfaces, the **Bridge** pattern aims to

decouple an abstraction from its implementation. This separation allows both sides—the abstraction and the concrete implementation(s)—to vary independently, promoting a system where changes in the abstraction do not necessarily force changes in the implementation and vice versa.

3.3.1 Context and Motivation

The Bridge pattern is especially valuable when you anticipate that your system will have **multiple variations** of an abstraction, each possibly requiring different implementations. For example, in a graphics application, you might have a Shape abstraction (circle, square, rectangle, etc.) that needs to be rendered using different **rendering APIs** (OpenGL, DirectX, Vulkan) or different **platform-** specific code. By implementing a bridge, you can combine any shape variant with any rendering approach without creating a combinatorial explosion of subclasses.

3.3.2 Structure and Participants

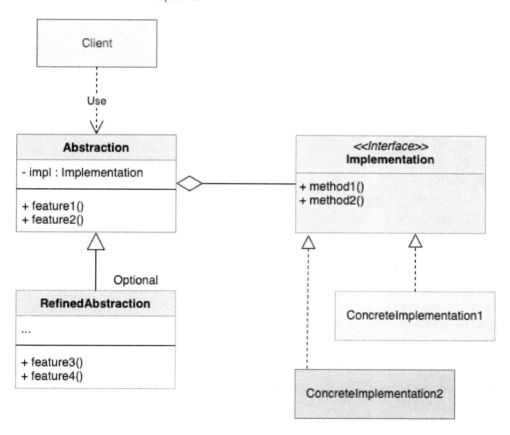

1. **Abstraction**: The high-level interface that clients interact with (e.g., Shape). Maintains a reference to an implementor.
2. **RefinedAbstraction**: A specialized abstraction that extends the base.
3. **Implementor**: The interface defining lower-level operations (e.g., Renderer).
4. **ConcreteImplementor**: Specific implementations (e.g., OpenGLRenderer,

47

DirectXRenderer).

3.3.3 Implementation Details

- **Prefer Composition over Inheritance**: The abstraction holds a reference to the implementor interface (object composition).

- **Implementation Variants**: You can add more ConcreteImplementors without affecting the abstraction.

- **Extended Hierarchy**: You can have multiple RefinedAbstractions as well.

Example (Pseudo-Code)

```
// Implementor
interface Renderer {
    void renderCircle(int x, int y, int radius);
    void renderRectangle(int x, int y, int width, int height);
}


// ConcreteImplementors
class OpenGLRenderer implements Renderer {
    @Override
    public void renderCircle(int x, int y, int radius) {
        System.out.println("OpenGL: Drawing circle at (" + x + ", " + y + "), radius " + radius);
    }
    @Override
    public void renderRectangle(int x, int y, int w, int h) {
        System.out.println("OpenGL: Drawing rectangle at (" + x + ", " + y + "), size " + w +
"x" + h);
    }
}


class DirectXRenderer implements Renderer {
    @Override
    public void renderCircle(int x, int y, int radius) {
        System.out.println("DirectX: Drawing circle at (" + x + ", " + y + "), radius " + radius);
    }
    @Override
    public void renderRectangle(int x, int y, int w, int h) {
        System.out.println("DirectX: Drawing rectangle at (" + x + ", " + y + "), size " + w +
"x" + h);
    }
}
```

```java
// Abstraction
abstract class Shape {
    protected Renderer renderer;

    protected Shape(Renderer renderer) {
        this.renderer = renderer;
    }

    public abstract void draw();
}

// Refined Abstractions
class Circle extends Shape {
    private int x, y, radius;

    public Circle(int x, int y, int r, Renderer renderer) {
        super(renderer);
        this.x = x;
        this.y = y;
        this.radius = r;
    }

    @Override
    public void draw() {
        renderer.renderCircle(x, y, radius);
    }
}

class Rectangle extends Shape {
    private int x, y, width, height;

    public Rectangle(int x, int y, int w, int h, Renderer renderer) {
        super(renderer);
        this.x = x;
        this.y = y;
        this.width = w;
        this.height = h;
    }
```

```
@Override
public void draw() {
    renderer.renderRectangle(x, y, width, height);
  }
}
```

3.3.4 Advantages and Disadvantages

- **Advantages**:
    o Separates abstraction interface from the implementation details.
    o Both abstraction and implementation hierarchies can grow independently.
    o Reduces code duplication by sharing an implementor among multiple abstractions.
- **Disadvantages**:
    o Introduces complexity through additional layers.
    o Requires careful design to ensure the bridging interfaces are stable and flexible enough.

3.3.5 Real-World Examples

- **File I/O**: An abstraction for file reading/writing with multiple implementors for local files, network files, or encrypted files.
- **Cross-Platform GUIs**: A widget abstraction and multiple platform-specific backends.
- **Persistence Layers**: An abstraction for data operations (CRUD) and multiple concrete data stores (SQL, NoSQL, in-memory).

3.4 Composite Pattern

The **Composite** pattern helps treat **individual objects** and **compositions of objects** in a uniform manner. It is particularly useful when dealing with **hierarchical** or **tree** structures, where nodes may themselves be made up of other nodes.

3.4.1 Context and Motivation

Consider a scenario where your system handles a file system with directories and files. A file is a leaf node, while a directory contains other files or directories. From the client's perspective, you might want a uniform interface—**open()**, **delete()**, **displayProperties()**, etc.—on both files and directories. Composite simplifies this by allowing you to call the same method on either a leaf or a container, letting each handle the request appropriately.

3.4.2 Structure and Participants

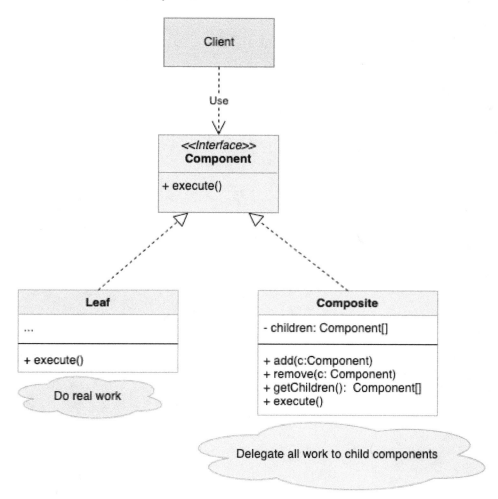

1. **Component**: Declares common operations for both simple (Leaf) and complex (Composite) objects.
2. **Leaf**: Represents end objects, with no children. Implements operations specifically.
3. **Composite**: Represents a node with children (also of type Component). Delivers or delegates tasks to children as needed.

3.4.3 Implementation Details

-   **Common Interface**: Both leaves and composites share a unified interface, e.g., draw(), calculateSize(), execute(), etc.
-   **Child Management Methods**: The composite typically provides methods like addChild(Component c) or removeChild(Component c). Leaves either do not implement these or implement them as no-ops (or throw exceptions).
-   **Recursive Behavior**: A composite calls the same methods on its children, enabling nested structures.

Example (Pseudo-Code)

```
interface FileSystemComponent {
   void showDetails();
}

class FileLeaf implements FileSystemComponent {
   private String name;
   public FileLeaf(String name) {
      this.name = name;
   }
   @Override
   public void showDetails() {
      System.out.println("File: " + name);
   }
}

class DirectoryComposite implements FileSystemComponent {
   private String name;
   private List<FileSystemComponent> children = new ArrayList<>();

   public DirectoryComposite(String name) {
      this.name = name;
   }

   public void add(FileSystemComponent component) {
      children.add(component);
   }

   public void remove(FileSystemComponent component) {
      children.remove(component);
   }

   @Override
   public void showDetails() {
      System.out.println("Directory: " + name);
      for(FileSystemComponent child : children) {
         child.showDetails();
      }
```

```
    }
  }
```

3.4.4 Advantages and Disadvantages

- **Advantages**:
    - o   Simplifies client code by treating individual items and collections uniformly.
    - o   Supports **arbitrary nesting** of child objects.
    - o   Makes it easier to add new kinds of components, as they just implement the existing interface.
- **Disadvantages**:
    - o   Can become overly general if forced on a system that doesn't require hierarchical or uniform treatment.
    - o   May complicate operations that should behave differently for leaves vs. composites if not carefully handled.

3.4.5 Real-World Examples

- **GUI component trees**: Buttons, panels, windows can be nested.
- **Organization charts**: Employees can be managers containing other employees or leaf-level staff.
- **XML/HTML document structures**: Elements that contain child elements or text nodes.

3.5 Decorator Pattern

The **Decorator** pattern allows you to add functionality to objects **dynamically**, without modifying their code or creating extensive subclasses. It "wraps" an object in a new class that implements the same interface, forwarding most calls while optionally adding or modifying behavior.

3.5.1 Context and Motivation

Inheritance can be used to extend class functionality, but it is a static relationship set at compile time and can quickly lead to an explosion of subclasses if you want many combinations of features. Decorator addresses this issue by enabling **runtime** composition. For instance, consider a text editor that can highlight text, add line numbers, or support spell-check. You can have a base TextEditor object, and apply "decorations" for each feature, layering multiple decorators as needed.

3.5.2 Structure and Participants

1. **Component**: Defines the interface for objects that can have responsibilities added dynamically.
2. **ConcreteComponent**: The base implementation, to which additional features are "decorated."
3. **Decorator**: Has a reference to a Component. Implements the same interface, forwarding calls to the wrapped component.
4. **ConcreteDecorator**: Adds or modifies behaviors before or after calling the wrapped component.

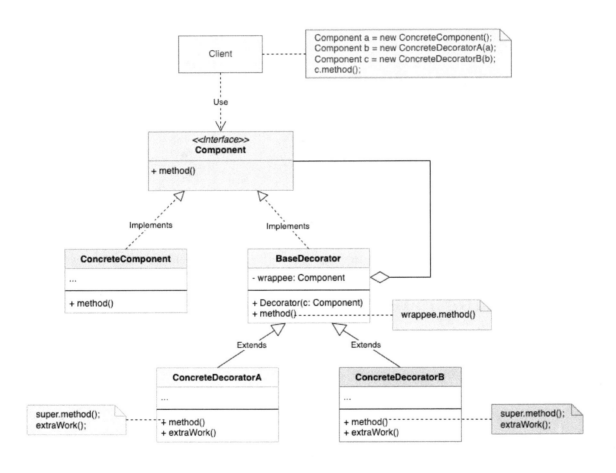

3.5.3 Implementation Details

- **Layering Decorators**: You can wrap a component in multiple decorators, each adding new behavior.
- **Transparent vs. Opaque Decorator**: Some decorators might keep the interface identical so that the client cannot tell it's wrapped, while others might introduce new methods (less common).

- **Performance Considerations**: Multiple layers of decorators can add overhead if the chain is long.

Example (Pseudo-Code)

```
// Component interface
interface TextSource {
   String getText();
}


// Concrete Component
class BasicText implements TextSource {
   private String text;
   public BasicText(String text) {
      this.text = text;
   }
   @Override
   public String getText() {
      return text;
   }
}


// Decorator
abstract class TextDecorator implements TextSource {
   protected TextSource wrappee;
   public TextDecorator(TextSource source) {
      this.wrappee = source;
   }
   @Override
   public String getText() {
      return wrappee.getText(); // default forwarding
   }
}

// Concrete Decorators
class UpperCaseDecorator extends TextDecorator {
   public UpperCaseDecorator(TextSource source) {
      super(source);
   }
   @Override
```

```java
    public String getText() {
        return super.getText().toUpperCase();
    }
}

class MarkdownDecorator extends TextDecorator {
    public MarkdownDecorator(TextSource source) {
        super(source);
    }
    @Override
    public String getText() {
        String text = super.getText();
        // naive example: wrap with some markdown formatting
        return "**" + text + "**";
    }
}

// Usage
class TextEditor {
    public static void main(String[] args) {
        TextSource text = new BasicText("hello decorator");
        text = new UpperCaseDecorator(text);
        text = new MarkdownDecorator(text);
        System.out.println(text.getText()); // prints "**HELLO DECORATOR**"
    }
}
```

3.5.4 Advantages and Disadvantages

- **Advantages**:
    - o Flexible alternative to subclassing.
    - o Responsibilities can be added or removed at runtime.
    - o Each decorator focuses on one additional behavior, encouraging single responsibility.
- **Disadvantages**:
    - o Can introduce complexity with many small objects if overused.
    - o The order of decorators can matter, which might confuse maintainers.
    - o Can be harder to debug due to multiple layers.

- **Java I/O Streams** (e.g., FileInputStream wrapped by BufferedInputStream wrapped by DataInputStream).
- **UI Components** that add scroll bars, borders, or other features by wrapping a base component.
- **Formatting/Logging** pipelines where each decorator adds a new step (e.g., encryption, compression).

3.6 Facade Pattern

When a subsystem becomes too complex or has numerous classes and interactions, a **Facade** provides a simpler, unified interface. The Facade delegates client requests to appropriate subsystem classes while shielding the client from the subsystem's internal complexity.

3.6.1 Context and Motivation

Large-scale systems often evolve over time, accumulating a variety of classes, modules, and utilities. A new developer or an external client might find it daunting to learn every detail to accomplish common tasks. The Facade pattern offers a higher-level entry point that orchestrates the underlying components. This approach can prevent the rest of the system from becoming tightly coupled to the subsystem's intricacies, improving maintainability and clarity.

3.6.2 Structure and Participants

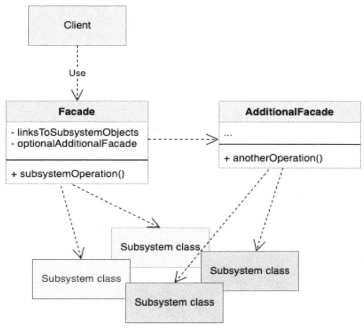

1. **Facade**: Offers a simplified interface to clients. Maintains references to relevant subsystem objects.
2. **Subsystem Classes**: Do the actual work. They do not usually have any reference to the facade—they operate with or without it.

3.6.3 Implementation Details

- **Aggregation of Services**: The facade might call multiple subsystem components in a single method, presenting a streamlined "one-stop shop" to the client.
- **No Additional Logic**: A facade typically should not add domain logic of its own. It's best to keep it as a "wrapper" or "entry point" that delegates appropriately.
- **Multiple Facades**: A system may have multiple facades targeting different subsets of functionality.

Example (Pseudo-Code)

```
class CompilerFacade {
    private LexicalAnalyzer lex;
    private Parser parser;
    private CodeGenerator codeGen;

    public CompilerFacade() {
        this.lex = new LexicalAnalyzer();
        this.parser = new Parser();
        this.codeGen = new CodeGenerator();
    }

    public void compile(String sourceCode) {
        TokenStream tokens = lex.tokenize(sourceCode);
        AST syntaxTree = parser.parse(tokens);
        byte[] machineCode = codeGen.generate(syntaxTree);
        System.out.println("Compilation done: " + machineCode.length + " bytes produced.");
    }
}

// Subsystem classes
class LexicalAnalyzer {
    public TokenStream tokenize(String source) { /* ... */ }
}
```

```
class Parser {
    public AST parse(TokenStream tokens) { /* ... */ }
}
class CodeGenerator {
    public byte[] generate(AST syntaxTree) { /* ... */ }
}

// Client usage
class IDE {
    public static void main(String[] args) {
        CompilerFacade compiler = new CompilerFacade();
        compiler.compile("print 'Hello facade';");
    }
}
```

3.6.4 Advantages and Disadvantages

- **Advantages**:
    - o Simplifies usage of a complex subsystem.
    - o Decouples client code from subsystem details.
    - o Provides a consistent interface, even if subsystem changes internally.
- **Disadvantages**:
    - o Over-simplification might restrict access to advanced subsystem features.
    - o Encourages a monolithic entry point if not designed carefully, which can become a bottleneck.

3.6.5 Real-World Examples

- **Library APIs**: Many frameworks present a facade class with static or top-level methods that handle complex library operations.
- **Toolkits**: A single class that orchestrates multiple components (e.g., rendering engines, network modules, etc.).
- **Transaction Scripts** in enterprise applications may orchestrate multiple domain objects via a façade to keep the UI layer simpler.

3.7 Flyweight Pattern

The **Flyweight** pattern minimizes memory usage (and sometimes processing overhead) by **sharing** as much data as possible among similar objects. When a system needs a large number of fine-grained objects—many of which have identical or nearly identical data—Flyweight steps in to share that data instead of duplicating it.

3.7.1 Context and Motivation

A classic example is rendering large text documents or GUIs with numerous repeated characters or icons. If each character or icon were a distinct object with its own identical data, memory usage would explode. Instead, with Flyweight, the data that can be shared (such as character glyph shapes) is stored once. Each "instance" is then either a reference to the shared data plus some **extrinsic** state specific to that instance (like position on the screen).

3.7.2 Structure and Participants

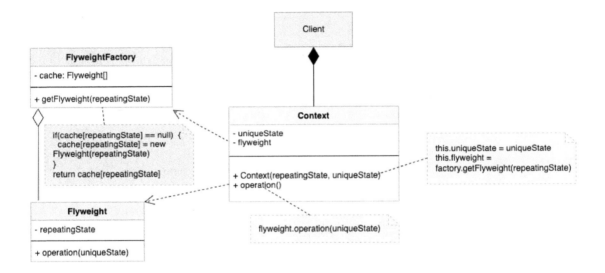

1. **Flyweight**: Declares a method accepting **extrinsic** data (context) that changes from one instance to another.
2. **ConcreteFlyweight**: Stores **intrinsic** data that can be shared.
3. **FlyweightFactory**: Creates and manages flyweight objects, ensuring clients reuse objects with the same intrinsic state.

3.7.3 Implementation Details

- **Intrinsic vs. Extrinsic State:**
    - **Intrinsic** data: Shared among multiple contexts, does not change (e.g., shape of a character glyph).
    - **Extrinsic** data: Varies per usage (e.g., position, color). It is kept outside the flyweight or passed in via method arguments.

- **Keys or Hashing**: The factory often uses a hash map or dictionary keyed by the intrinsic data to retrieve or create the shared objects.

Example (Pseudo-Code)

```java
// Flyweight interface
interface Glyph {
    void draw(int x, int y);  // x, y are extrinsic context
}


// ConcreteFlyweight
class CharacterGlyph implements Glyph {
    private char character;  // intrinsic

    public CharacterGlyph(char c) {
        this.character = c;
    }


    @Override
    public void draw(int x, int y) {
        // Use 'character' to lookup shape or do something
        // x,y is the extrinsic data
        System.out.println("Drawing character '" + character + "' at (" + x + "," + y + ")");
    }
}

// Flyweight Factory
class GlyphFactory {
    private Map<Character, Glyph> cache = new HashMap<>();

    public Glyph getGlyph(char c) {
        if (!cache.containsKey(c)) {
            cache.put(c, new CharacterGlyph(c));
        }
        return cache.get(c);
    }
}

// Usage
class TextEditor {
```

```
    public static void main(String[] args) {
        String text = "hello flyweight";
        GlyphFactory factory = new GlyphFactory();
        int xPosition = 0;
        for(char c : text.toCharArray()) {
            Glyph glyph = factory.getGlyph(c);
            glyph.draw(xPosition, 0);
            xPosition += 10; // next character
        }
    }
}
```

3.7.4 Advantages and Disadvantages

- **Advantages**:
  - o Substantial memory savings for large numbers of similar objects.
  - o Centralized management of shared data, leading to consistent usage.
  - o Potential performance gains in certain contexts (less duplication to manage).
- **Disadvantages**:
  - o More complexity, as extrinsic data must be managed externally.
  - o Not useful if the objects in question do not share significant amounts of data.
  - o Overhead in retrieving or computing extrinsic state at runtime.

3.7.5 Real-World Examples

- **Text editors**: Managing glyphs for each character.
- **Map or tile-based games**: Reusing the same tile data across large game maps.
- **GUI icons**: Large sets of identical or similar icon images used in many places.

3.8 Proxy Pattern

A **Proxy** provides a surrogate or placeholder for another object, controlling access to it. The proxy typically implements the same interface as its real subject but adds logic—such as lazy initialization, access control, logging, or remote communication—before delegating to the actual object.

3.8.1 Context and Motivation

Proxies arise in several contexts:

- **Remote Proxy**: The actual object resides on a different machine or network location; the proxy handles communication details.

- **Virtual Proxy**: An expensive object is not created until truly needed. The proxy may hold minimal data and create the real object on demand.
- **Protection Proxy**: Controls access to the real object, possibly based on user roles or permissions.
- **Caching Proxy**: Reuses the results of expensive operations.

3.8.2 Structure and Participants

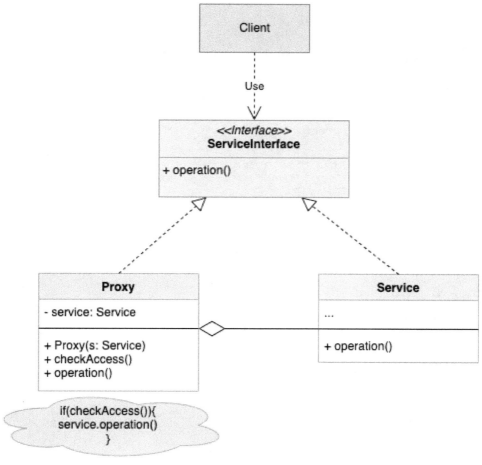

1. **Subject**: Common interface for the real object and the proxy.
2. **RealSubject**: The actual, core object that performs the business logic.
3. **Proxy**: Implements the same interface as the RealSubject. Manages access, logging, caching, or other additional concerns.

3.8.3 Implementation Details

- **Reference to RealSubject**: The proxy typically holds a reference, which might be dynamically created, or lazily initialized.

- **Method Interception**: The proxy methods do their additional logic before or after delegating the call to the real object.
- **Proxy Variants**:
  - **Remote Proxy**: Manages serialization, network calls, etc.
  - **Virtual Proxy**: Creates the real object when needed.
  - **Protection Proxy**: Checks credentials or contexts before delegation.

Example (Pseudo-Code)

```
// Subject
interface Image {
   void display();
}

// RealSubject
class HighResImage implements Image {
   private String filename;

   public HighResImage(String filename) {
      this.filename = filename;
      loadImageFromDisk(); // expensive operation
   }

   private void loadImageFromDisk() {
      System.out.println("Loading high-res image from disk: " + filename);
   }

   @Override
   public void display() {
      System.out.println("Displaying high-res image: " + filename);
   }
}

// Proxy
class ImageProxy implements Image {
   private String filename;
   private HighResImage realImage;

   public ImageProxy(String filename) {
      this.filename = filename;
```

```
    }

    @Override
    public void display() {
      if(realImage == null) {
        realImage = new HighResImage(filename);
      }
      realImage.display();
    }
}

// Usage
class PhotoViewer {
    public static void main(String[] args) {
      Image img = new ImageProxy("large_photo.jpg");
      // The real image isn't loaded yet
      img.display();
      // Now the real image loads and displays
    }
}
```

3.8.4 Advantages and Disadvantages

- **Advantages**:
  - o Manages resource usage (lazy loading), security (protection checks), or remote calls (transparency to client).
  - o Keeps client code unchanged while introducing new behaviors or optimizations.
- **Disadvantages**:
  - o Adds a level of indirection, which can obscure debugging.
  - o Proxy must accurately mirror the RealSubject's interface.
  - o In concurrency-intensive scenarios, synchronization complexities may arise.

3.8.5 Real-World Examples

- **Lazy loading** of large images or files in user interfaces.
- **Remote method invocation** frameworks, where local proxies represent remote objects.
- **Access control** for domain objects in enterprise applications, restricting certain methods or data based on roles.

3.9 Comparing Structural Patterns

Having explored each structural pattern, it's useful to map out how they differ, so you can choose the right one for specific scenarios.

Pattern	Purpose	Key Distinctions
Adapter	Convert one interface into another so that classes can work together.	Focuses on **interface conversion**; a wrapper that modifies the interface.
Bridge	Separate abstraction from implementation to allow both to vary independently.	Ideal for an evolving hierarchy: **decouples** the high-level logic from platform-specific or detail-level logic.
Composite	Represent part-whole hierarchies, letting clients treat individual objects and compositions uniformly.	Best for **tree** structures with uniform methods.
Decorator	Add responsibilities to an object dynamically without affecting others.	A **wrap** that modifies behavior at runtime, *without* altering the original code.
Facade	Provide a simplified interface to a complex subsystem.	**Reduces complexity** by offering a top-level interface, but doesn't hide the subsystem from advanced users if direct access is needed.
Flyweight	Share objects to support large numbers of similar objects efficiently.	Manages **intrinsic** vs. **extrinsic** data to conserve memory. Often used for repeated small items like characters in text.
Proxy	Provide a surrogate or placeholder to control access to another object.	Often used for **lazy loading**, remote access, or security checks.

3.10 Common Pitfalls and Best Practices for Structural Patterns

When choosing and implementing structural patterns, engineers should be aware of certain pitfalls and recommended best practices:

1. **Overuse of Wrappers (Decorator, Proxy, Adapter)**
   - **Pitfall**: Nested wrappers can become difficult to debug or reason about, especially if multiple layers do different transformations.
   - **Best Practice**: Keep wrapping chains short and well-documented. Consider if a simpler approach or a single façade might suffice for minor interface mismatches.

2. **Unnecessary Abstraction (Bridge)**
   - **Pitfall**: Introducing a Bridge where there is no real need for separate abstraction and implementation hierarchies leads to complexity with minimal benefit.
   - **Best Practice**: Implement a Bridge when you foresee multiple variations of both the abstraction and the underlying implementation.

3. **Incorrect Layering in Composite**
   - **Pitfall**: If some child nodes have drastically different behaviors or require unique operations, forcing them into a single interface can lead to confusion.
   - **Best Practice**: Ensure that all child nodes truly share enough commonality to make the Composite pattern valuable.

4. **Shallow vs. Deep Subsystem Wrapping with Facade**
   - **Pitfall**: A façade that simply re-exposes each subsystem method doesn't truly simplify anything. Conversely, an overly simplistic façade may omit essential features.
   - **Best Practice**: Let the façade orchestrate typical usage scenarios. It shouldn't replicate every subsystem method but offer higher-level operations. Provide advanced clients direct access to the subsystem if needed.

5. **Memory vs. CPU Trade-offs in Flyweight**
   - **Pitfall**: Maintaining a large factory or a complex approach to extrinsic data can degrade performance if your usage pattern doesn't truly benefit from shared state.
   - **Best Practice**: Carefully assess the memory usage and overhead of retrieving extrinsic data. If the overhead is higher than the memory savings, Flyweight might be counterproductive.

6. **Proxy Synchronization and Concurrency**
   - **Pitfall**: When proxies do additional work (e.g., caching, security checks), concurrency issues might arise if multiple threads access the proxy.
   - **Best Practice**: Consider thread safety from the start. Use locks, thread-safe data structures, or stateless proxies that delegate each call safely.

3.11 Real-World Scenarios Integrating Multiple Structural Patterns

In many enterprise or large-scale applications, you might find **multiple structural patterns** working together:

1. **Modern Web Framework**
   - **Adapter** for integrating third-party modules whose interfaces differ from the application's internal standards.
   - **Facade** to present a cohesive controller/service interface for complex domain logic (hiding multiple domain objects).
   - **Decorator** for adding cross-cutting concerns like security checks or data validation to requests on the fly.

2. **Large-Scale Game Engine**
   - **Composite** for the scene graph (nested game objects, lights, cameras).
   - **Flyweight** for repeated assets like repeated model textures or identical entities (e.g., thousands of identical particles).
   - **Proxy** for remote or networked objects in multiplayer contexts.

3. **Graphics Rendering Pipeline**
   - **Bridge** for decoupling shape or object definitions from a specific rendering API (OpenGL vs. Vulkan).
   - **Facade** presenting a single API to client code, while behind the scenes it calls multiple libraries for resource loading, shader compilation, etc.
   - **Decorator** for adding special effects (post-processing, shading) to existing objects at runtime.

Chapter 4: Behavioral Design Patterns

Software often involves dynamic interactions among various objects. These interactions can be intricate: determining who handles a request, how a user command is executed or undone, how an object notifies many others about a change, how an algorithm's steps are organized, and so on. **Behavioral design patterns** streamline these interactions by defining common approaches that keep responsibilities well-structured, reduce coupling, and facilitate extensions or modifications.

4.1 Overview of Behavioral Patterns

Behavioral patterns address problems such as:

- **Responsibility Management**: Which object or set of objects is responsible for handling a request? How can we prevent a single object from becoming a bottleneck?
- **Communication Channels**: How do objects collaborate while staying loosely coupled? How do they notify each other without forming tangled webs of dependencies?
- **Flexibility in Algorithms**: In scenarios where you want to vary an algorithm's steps or easily swap out different strategies, how do you do so cleanly?
- **Object State and Transitions**: Complex objects might change behaviors based on their internal state. How do you structure such logic without massive if-else chains?

By employing the correct behavioral pattern, you can keep your code more readable, more testable, and easier to maintain. Let's examine each pattern in detail.

4.2 Chain of Responsibility Pattern

The **Chain of Responsibility** pattern decouples **senders** of a request from potential **receivers**, allowing multiple objects a chance to handle the request before it either completes or traverses the entire chain unhandled. This pattern often appears in event-handling systems or systems where requests might be passed through a series of filters or validators.

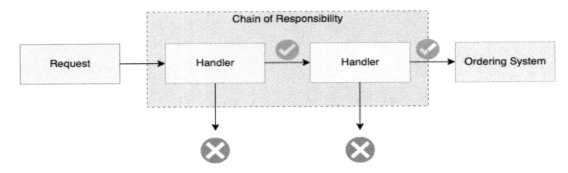

4.2.1 Context and Motivation

Imagine a **support ticket** system where incoming requests may be handled by various levels of support staff—Level 1, Level 2, Level 3. If Level 1 support can't solve it, the ticket is escalated up the chain. The sender need only submit the ticket; it doesn't need to know which level of support can solve it.

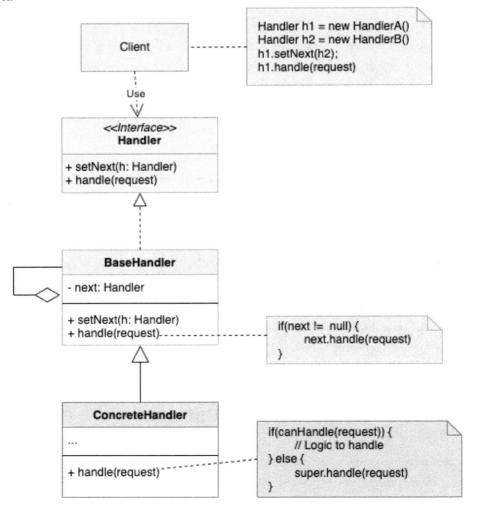

Alternatively, consider an **UI event** in a GUI framework—clicks or keystrokes might bubble up from a child widget to parent containers if the child doesn't handle them, eventually reaching a top-level object.

This pattern keeps request-handling logic distributed among classes that have the potential to handle it, avoiding a centralized manager or cumbersome if-else statements that try every possible approach.

4.2.2 Structure and Participants

Handler: Declares a method for handling the request (e.g., handleRequest()) and optionally references the next handler in the chain.

1. **ConcreteHandler**: Implements the request handling. If it can handle the request, it does so; otherwise, it passes it along.
2. **Client**: Initiates the request, typically through the first handler in the chain.

4.2.3 Implementation Details

- **Building the Chain**:
    - o You can link handlers either statically (in code) or dynamically (e.g., reading configuration that sets up the chain).
- **Termination**:
    - o If no handler can process the request, the request typically "falls off" the chain or returns a default outcome.
- **Single or Multiple Handlers**:
    - o The chain can end once the first capable handler processes the request, or it can continue letting multiple handlers act.

Example (Pseudo-Code)

```
abstract class HelpHandler {
  protected HelpHandler nextHandler;

  public void setNext(HelpHandler handler) {
    this.nextHandler = handler;
  }

  public void handleHelp(String topic) {
    if (nextHandler != null) {
      nextHandler.handleHelp(topic);
```

```java
      }
    }
  }

class BasicHelpHandler extends HelpHandler {
  @Override
  public void handleHelp(String topic) {
    if (topic.equals("basic")) {
      System.out.println("Showing basic help...");
    } else {
      super.handleHelp(topic);
    }
  }
}

class AdvancedHelpHandler extends HelpHandler {
  @Override
  public void handleHelp(String topic) {
    if (topic.equals("advanced")) {
      System.out.println("Showing advanced help...");
    } else {
      super.handleHelp(topic);
    }
  }
}

// Client sets up chain
class Application {
  public static void main(String[] args) {
    HelpHandler basic = new BasicHelpHandler();
    HelpHandler advanced = new AdvancedHelpHandler();
    basic.setNext(advanced);

    // The client only knows to call basic
    basic.handleHelp("basic");
    basic.handleHelp("advanced");
    basic.handleHelp("unknown");
  }
}
```

4.2.4 Advantages and Disadvantages

- **Advantages**:
    - o Reduces coupling between sender and receivers.
    - o Flexibility in assigning responsibilities; easy to add or remove handlers or rearrange the chain.
    - o Encourages single responsibility for each handler.
- **Disadvantages**:
    - o May lead to unhandled requests if no receiver handles them, unless carefully managed.
    - o Tracing a request's path can be tricky if the chain is long.

4.2.5 Real-World Examples

- **Logging frameworks**: multiple appenders that handle log messages in turn.
- **UI event bubbling**: from child widget to parent containers.
- **Servlet filters** in Java web apps, or middleware chains in frameworks like Express.js.

4.3 Command Pattern

The **Command** pattern encapsulates a request (an operation and its arguments) as an object, decoupling the client invoking the operation from the object that performs it. This pattern also supports features like **undo/redo**, logging, or queuing commands for execution at a later time.

4.3.1 Context and Motivation

Think of a text editor with an "undo" function. Each user action—typing text, formatting, deleting—should be reversible. One approach: whenever the user performs an action, store that action as a **Command** object which knows how to undo itself. The system can hold these command objects in a stack, popping and executing "undo" when required.

Another context is an **execution queue**. The Command pattern allows you to separate the creation of an operation from its execution, enabling you to queue commands, schedule them, or distribute them across different execution threads.

4.3.2 Structure and Participants

1. **Command**: Declares the interface for executing an action, often with optional undo/redo methods.
2. **ConcreteCommand**: Implements the specifics of the operation, typically referencing a **Receiver** that actually does the work.

3. **Receiver**: Has the knowledge to perform the request's action(s).
4. **Invoker**: The object (like a UI button) that triggers the command's execute() method.
5. **Client**: Instantiates and configures ConcreteCommand objects.

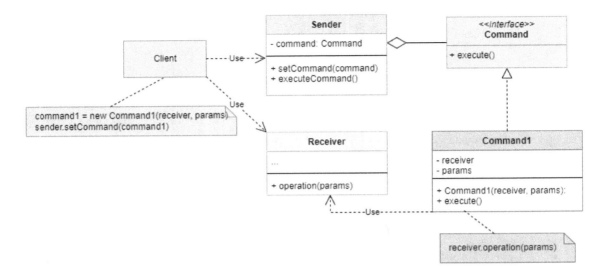

4.3.3 Implementation Details

- **Undo/Redo**: A command can store state needed to revert an operation.
- **Multiple Receivers**: A single command can coordinate actions across multiple receivers if needed.
- **Command History**: The system might keep a list or stack of executed commands to revert them in reverse order.

Example (Pseudo-Code)

```
interface Command {
    void execute();
    void undo();
}


// Receiver
class TextDocument {
    private StringBuilder content = new StringBuilder();

    public void append(String text) {
        content.append(text);
    }
    public void removeLast(int length) {
```

```java
      int start = content.length() - length;
      content.delete(start, start + length);
    }
    public String getContent() {
      return content.toString();
    }
}


// ConcreteCommand
class AppendCommand implements Command {
    private TextDocument doc;
    private String textToAppend;
    private int appendedLength;

    public AppendCommand(TextDocument doc, String text) {
      this.doc = doc;
      this.textToAppend = text;
    }

    @Override
    public void execute() {
      doc.append(textToAppend);
      appendedLength = textToAppend.length();
    }

    @Override
    public void undo() {
      doc.removeLast(appendedLength);
    }
}


// Invoker
class TextEditor {
    private Stack<Command> history = new Stack<>();

    public void executeCommand(Command cmd) {
      cmd.execute();
      history.push(cmd);
    }
```

```java
    public void undoLast() {
        if(!history.isEmpty()) {
            Command cmd = history.pop();
            cmd.undo();
        }
    }
}

// Client usage
class ClientApp {
    public static void main(String[] args) {
        TextDocument doc = new TextDocument();
        TextEditor editor = new TextEditor();

        Command cmd1 = new AppendCommand(doc, "Hello ");
        Command cmd2 = new AppendCommand(doc, "World!");

        editor.executeCommand(cmd1);
        editor.executeCommand(cmd2);

        System.out.println(doc.getContent()); // "Hello World!"

        editor.undoLast();
        System.out.println(doc.getContent()); // "Hello "
    }
}
```

4.3.4 Advantages and Disadvantages

- **Advantages**:
    - o Decouples object invoking the operation from the one performing it.
    - o Enables easy support for **undo**, **redo**, **logging**, or **queuing**.
    - o Composes complex operations from simpler commands.
- **Disadvantages**:
    - o Potential for a large number of command classes if the application has many distinct operations.
    - o Storing state for undo can be memory-intensive.

- **GUI actions**: Clicking a button in a text editor often triggers a Command.
- **Remote method invocation**: Each invocation can be represented as a command object.
- **Macros**: Grouping multiple commands into a single higher-level operation.

4.4 Interpreter Pattern

The **Interpreter** pattern defines a representation of a language's grammar and uses that representation to **interpret** sentences in the language. Each rule in the grammar corresponds to a class, and parsing/evaluation traverses a structure of these rule classes.

4.4.1 Context and Motivation

This pattern is ideal when you need to implement **simple scripting or domain-specific languages** (DSLs). For example, if you have a system that needs to evaluate expressions like A AND B or parse a simple math expression syntax. Instead of writing a full-blown parser or leveraging external libraries, the Interpreter pattern organizes grammar rules into a class structure that can interpret expressions directly in code.

4.4.2 Structure and Participants

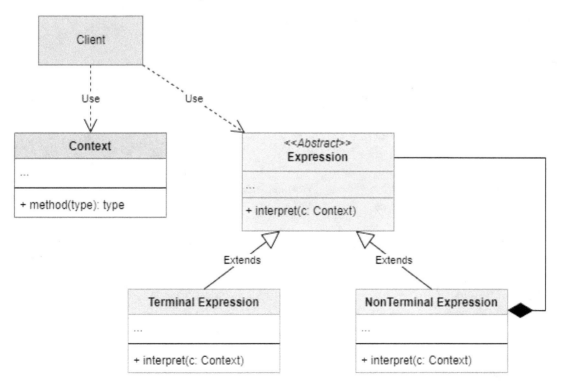

1. **AbstractExpression**: Declares an interpret(context) method.
2. **TerminalExpression**: Represents a leaf node in the grammar (e.g., a variable or a number).
3. **NonterminalExpression**: Composes multiple expressions to interpret more complex rules (e.g., addition, AND operations, etc.).
4. **Context**: Contains input data or the state needed for interpretation (e.g., a symbol table).

4.4.3 Implementation Details

- **Grammar Representation**: Each class corresponds to a grammar production rule.
- **Parse Tree**: Typically, you build a parse tree for an input expression, then call interpret() on the root.
- **Limited Use Cases**: If the grammar is large or complex, a dedicated parser generator might be more appropriate than the Interpreter pattern.

Example (Pseudo-Code)

A simple boolean expression interpreter:

```
interface BooleanExpression {
    boolean interpret(Map<String, Boolean> context);
}

// Terminal expression
class Variable implements BooleanExpression {
    private String name;

    public Variable(String name) {
        this.name = name;
    }

    @Override
    public boolean interpret(Map<String, Boolean> context) {
        return context.get(name);
    }
}

// Non-terminal expressions
class AndExpression implements BooleanExpression {
    private BooleanExpression expr1, expr2;
    public AndExpression(BooleanExpression expr1, BooleanExpression expr2) {
        this.expr1 = expr1;
```

```java
        this.expr2 = expr2;
    }
    @Override
    public boolean interpret(Map<String, Boolean> context) {
        return expr1.interpret(context) && expr2.interpret(context);
    }
}

class OrExpression implements BooleanExpression {
    private BooleanExpression expr1, expr2;
    public OrExpression(BooleanExpression expr1, BooleanExpression expr2) {
        this.expr1 = expr1;
        this.expr2 = expr2;
    }
    @Override
    public boolean interpret(Map<String, Boolean> context) {
        return expr1.interpret(context) || expr2.interpret(context);
    }
}

// Usage
class InterpreterDemo {
    public static void main(String[] args) {
        BooleanExpression varA = new Variable("A");
        BooleanExpression varB = new Variable("B");

        BooleanExpression expression = new AndExpression(varA, new OrExpression(varA, varB));
        Map<String, Boolean> context = new HashMap<>();
        context.put("A", true);
        context.put("B", false);

        System.out.println(expression.interpret(context)); // true && (true || false) => true
    }
}
```

4.4.4 Advantages and Disadvantages

- **Advantages**:

79

- o Makes grammar more explicit in code.
- o Easy to extend or modify small grammars.
- o Each rule is a class, which can be tested independently.
- **Disadvantages**:
  - o Can lead to a large class hierarchy for complex grammars.
  - o Less efficient than using specialized parsing tools or interpreters for bigger languages.

4.4.5 Real-World Examples

- **Simple DSLs** embedded in an application, e.g., business rule evaluators.
- **Configuration expressions** that interpret custom syntax for user settings.
- **Math parser** for embedded calculators or expression engines.

4.5 Iterator Pattern

The **Iterator** pattern provides a way to **sequentially access** elements of a collection without exposing its internal representation. It decouples the logic of how elements are accessed from the underlying data structure, letting you swap out different collection types without altering client code that iterates over them.

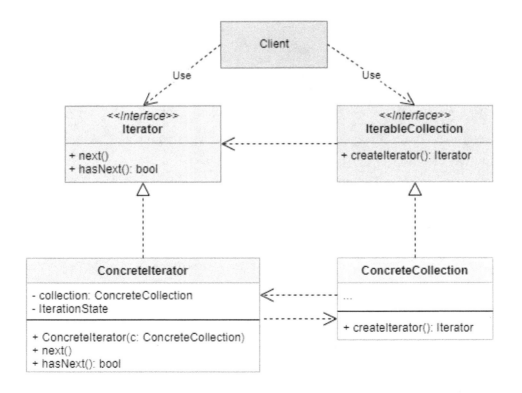

4.5.1 Context and Motivation

Whether you have a **list, tree, or graph**, client code often needs a uniform way to traverse items. Instead of scattering iteration logic across the client, the Iterator pattern encapsulates it within a specialized object called an **iterator**. This object has methods like hasNext(), next(), and optionally remove() for collection manipulation.

Many modern languages provide built-in iteration protocols (e.g., in Python, the __iter__ mechanism; in Java, the Iterator interface). Nonetheless, the pattern's conceptual value remains in clarifying how iteration can be abstracted from the data structure itself.

4.5.2 Structure and Participants

1. **Iterator**: Declares operations for traversing elements.
2. **ConcreteIterator**: Implements the iteration for a specific collection. Maintains its own iteration state (e.g., current index).
3. **Aggregate**: Declares a createIterator() method, returning an Iterator.
4. **ConcreteAggregate**: Stores elements; returns a suitable ConcreteIterator.

4.5.3 Implementation Details

- **Internal vs. External Iterators**:
  - **External**: The client controls the iteration (classic approach with hasNext(), next()).
  - **Internal**: The iterator controls the iteration, often by calling a callback for each element.
- **Multiple Iterators**: A collection can produce different iterators (e.g., forward, reverse) by returning different ConcreteIterator objects.
- **Fail-Fast Iteration**: Some modern iterations detect structural changes in the collection and fail fast to prevent inconsistent states.

Example (Pseudo-Code)

```
interface Iterator<T> {
   boolean hasNext();
   T next();
}

interface Collection<T> {
   Iterator<T> createIterator();
}
```

```java
// Concrete Aggregate
class BookCollection implements Collection<String> {
    private String[] books;

    public BookCollection(String[] books) {
        this.books = books;
    }

    @Override
    public Iterator<String> createIterator() {
        return new BookIterator(this);
    }

    public String getItem(int index) {
        return books[index];
    }

    public int size() {
        return books.length;
    }
}

// Concrete Iterator
class BookIterator implements Iterator<String> {
    private BookCollection collection;
    private int currentIndex = 0;

    public BookIterator(BookCollection collection) {
        this.collection = collection;
    }

    @Override
    public boolean hasNext() {
        return currentIndex < collection.size();
    }

    @Override
    public String next() {
        return collection.getItem(currentIndex++);
```

```
        }
    }

    // Usage
    class LibraryDemo {
        public static void main(String[] args) {
            BookCollection library = new BookCollection(new String[] {
                "Design Patterns", "Clean Code", "Refactoring"
            });
            Iterator<String> it = library.createIterator();
            while(it.hasNext()) {
                System.out.println(it.next());
            }
        }
    }
}
```

4.5.4 Advantages and Disadvantages

- **Advantages**:
    - o   Unifies how different collections are traversed.
    - o   Simplifies client code, as iteration logic is encapsulated.
    - o   Allows multiple simultaneous traversals.
- **Disadvantages**:
    - o   Can introduce overhead if an internal iteration protocol was simpler.
    - o   Requires additional classes (iterator objects) for each collection.

4.5.5 Real-World Examples

- **All modern collections** in Java, C++, C#, etc. support iterators.
- **Tree and graph traversal** libraries often define specialized iterators.
- **Database cursors** can be seen as a form of iterator over result sets.

4.6 Mediator Pattern

The **Mediator** pattern centralizes **complex communication** or **control flows** among multiple objects. Instead of letting each object communicate with others directly (creating a tangle of references and logic), objects talk to a **Mediator**, which orchestrates interactions.

4.6.1 Context and Motivation

Consider a user interface with multiple widgets (text fields, buttons, checkboxes) that need to update each other's state. If each widget updated every other widget directly, the codebase would become difficult to maintain. A **Mediator** can handle these interactions, letting widgets be simpler and more focused on their own functionality.

The pattern is also useful in systems where you have multiple colleagues or components that can produce events that must be coordinated. The Mediator ensures changes in one component properly reflect in others without them depending on each other explicitly.

4.6.2 Structure and Participants

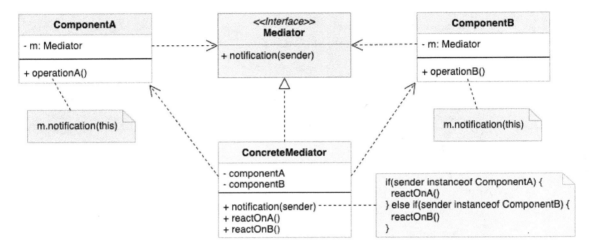

1. **Mediator**: Defines an interface for communicating with **Colleagues**.
2. **ConcreteMediator**: Implements cooperative behavior by coordinating colleagues, storing references, and handling interactions.
3. **Colleague**: Objects that collaborate with each other indirectly via the mediator.

4.6.3 Implementation Details

- **Registering Colleagues**: The mediator typically has references to all the colleagues it coordinates.
- **Event-Driven**: Often, a colleague notifies the mediator of an event; the mediator decides which other colleagues need to react, ensuring a clean separation of concerns.
- **Reduced Coupling**: Colleagues no longer need direct references to each other, making them more reusable.

Example (Pseudo-Code)

```
interface Mediator {
```

```java
    void notify(Component sender, String event);
}

abstract class Component {
    protected Mediator mediator;
    public void setMediator(Mediator mediator) {
        this.mediator = mediator;
    }
}

class Button extends Component {
    public void click() {
        // some logic
        mediator.notify(this, "click");
    }
}

class TextBox extends Component {
    private String text = "";

    public void setText(String t) {
        text = t;
        mediator.notify(this, "textChanged");
    }
    public String getText() { return text; }
}

// ConcreteMediator
class DialogMediator implements Mediator {
    private Button okButton;
    private TextBox input;

    public void setButton(Button b) { this.okButton = b; }
    public void setTextBox(TextBox t) { this.input = t; }

    @Override
    public void notify(Component sender, String event) {
        if (sender == okButton && event.equals("click")) {
            System.out.println("Button clicked. Submitting: " + input.getText());
```

```java
        } else if (sender == input && event.equals("textChanged")) {
            if (input.getText().isEmpty()) {
                System.out.println("Text is empty, disable button");
            } else {
                System.out.println("Text is present, enable button");
            }
        }
    }
}

// Usage
class App {
    public static void main(String[] args) {
        DialogMediator mediator = new DialogMediator();
        Button button = new Button();
        TextBox textBox = new TextBox();

        button.setMediator(mediator);
        textBox.setMediator(mediator);

        mediator.setButton(button);
        mediator.setTextBox(textBox);

        textBox.setText("Hello Mediator");
        button.click();
    }
}
```

4.6.4 Advantages and Disadvantages

- **Advantages**:
  - o Centralizes complex interactions, reducing coupling among colleagues.
  - o Simplifies maintenance, as you can extend or modify how components interact in one place (the mediator).
- **Disadvantages**:
  - o The mediator can become a **god object** if it grows too large, controlling too many interactions.
  - o If not carefully designed, the mediator's logic might become as complex as the code it was meant to simplify.

- **GUI libraries** with a dialog or form manager controlling multiple widgets.
- **Air traffic control**: A tower (mediator) coordinates planes (colleagues).
- **Chat rooms**: A chat server acts as a mediator among clients.

4.7 Memento Pattern

The **Memento** pattern captures an object's **internal state** without exposing its internals, allowing you to restore the object to this state later. It's commonly used for **undo** mechanisms or for saving snapshots of an object during its lifecycle.

4.7.1 Context and Motivation

When implementing **undo/redo**, you may need to revert an object to a previous state. If you stored that state externally, you might break encapsulation by accessing private fields. The Memento pattern solves this by having the object produce a **memento** containing its internal details, letting the caretaker hold onto it without peering inside.

4.7.2 Structure and Participants

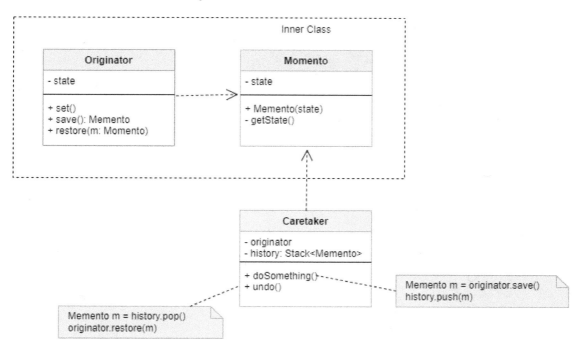

1. **Originator**: The object whose state you want to preserve/restore.
2. **Memento**: Holds the internal state. The **narrow interface** is what the Caretaker sees (just

a token), the **wide interface** is visible to the Originator, which can read/write its state.

3. **Caretaker**: Manages the memento's lifecycle. It never modifies the memento's content.

4.7.3 Implementation Details

- **Two Interfaces**:
    - o **Narrow** (public) to be used by the caretaker, which can't access state.
    - o **Wide** (private or protected) accessible by the originator, which can set or retrieve the internal data.
- **Snapshot vs. Incremental**: Some systems store the entire state in each memento, others store only diffs.

Example (Pseudo-Code)

```
class EditorState {
  private String content;
  public EditorState(String content) {
    this.content = content;
  }
  public String getContent() {
    return content;
  }
}

// Originator
class TextEditor {
  private String content = "";

  public void setContent(String c) {
    content = c;
  }

  public String getContent() {
    return content;
  }

  public EditorState createState() {
    return new EditorState(content);
  }
```

```java
    public void restore(EditorState state) {
        this.content = state.getContent();
    }
}

// Caretaker
class History {
    private Stack<EditorState> states = new Stack<>();

    public void push(EditorState state) {
        states.push(state);
    }
    public EditorState pop() {
        return states.pop();
    }
}

// Usage
class MementoDemo {
    public static void main(String[] args) {
        TextEditor editor = new TextEditor();
        History history = new History();

        editor.setContent("Hello");
        history.push(editor.createState());

        editor.setContent("Hello Memento");
        history.push(editor.createState());

        editor.setContent("Final text");
        editor.restore(history.pop()); // revert to "Hello Memento"
        System.out.println(editor.getContent());
    }
}
```

4.7.4 Advantages and Disadvantages

- **Advantages**:
    - Preserves encapsulation of the originator's state.

o Simplifies implementing **undo** functionality.

- **Disadvantages**:
  - o Can be memory intensive if state snapshots are large or if saved frequently.
  - o Doesn't handle external resources well if they aren't part of the object's state (e.g., file handles).

4.7.5 Real-World Examples

- **Text editors** with multiple levels of undo.
- **Graphics or gaming**: Saving a snapshot of a level or scene state.
- **Workflow** or **configuration** snapshots in enterprise apps.

4.8 Observer Pattern

The **Observer** pattern (sometimes called **Publish/Subscribe**) defines a **one-to-many** relationship where multiple observers automatically receive updates when a subject changes state. This pattern helps reduce coupling by letting subjects broadcast changes without explicitly calling methods on all observers.

4.8.1 Context and Motivation

Typical scenarios include **GUIs**: A data model changes, and multiple views need to update themselves. Another example is an **event bus** or stock ticker feed: the data source (subject) updates many subscribers. Instead of the subject having references to every observer, the Observer pattern forms a flexible subscription mechanism.

4.8.2 Structure and Participants

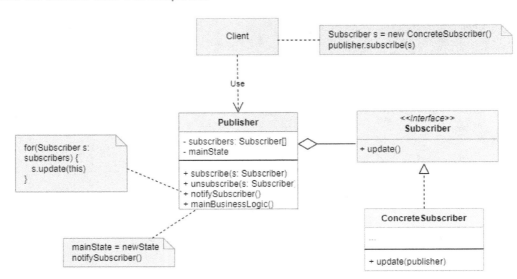

1. **Subject**: Keeps a list of observers and provides methods for adding/removing them. Provides a notify() method to update all observers about changes.
2. **Observer**: Declares an update() method, called by the subject.
3. **ConcreteSubject**: Maintains specific data (state) and notifies observers upon changes.
4. **ConcreteObserver**: Implements reaction to changes in the subject.

4.8.3 Implementation Details

- **Push vs. Pull Model**:
  - **Push**: The subject passes state to observers in notify().
  - **Pull**: Observers query the subject for updated data.
- **Broadcast vs. Specific**: The subject often calls update() for every observer. Observers might need to check whether the change affects them.
- **Multiple Subjects**: An observer can subscribe to multiple subjects.

Example (Pseudo-Code)

```
interface Observer {
   void update();
}

abstract class Subject {
   private List<Observer> observers = new ArrayList<>();

   public void attach(Observer obs) {
      observers.add(obs);
   }
   public void detach(Observer obs) {
      observers.remove(obs);
   }
   protected void notifyObservers() {
      for(Observer o : observers) {
         o.update();
      }
   }
}

// ConcreteSubject
class WeatherStation extends Subject {
```

```java
    private float temperature;

    public void setTemperature(float temp) {
        this.temperature = temp;
        notifyObservers();
    }
    public float getTemperature() {
        return this.temperature;
    }
}


// ConcreteObserver
class Display implements Observer {
    private WeatherStation station;

    public Display(WeatherStation ws) {
        this.station = ws;
    }

    @Override
    public void update() {
        System.out.println("Display updated: Temperature is " + station.getTemperature());
    }
}


// Usage
class ObserverDemo {
    public static void main(String[] args) {
        WeatherStation station = new WeatherStation();
        Display display1 = new Display(station);
        station.attach(display1);

        station.setTemperature(25.0f);
        station.setTemperature(30.0f);
    }
}
```

4.8.4 Advantages and Disadvantages

- **Advantages**:
  - o Decouples subject and observers. Additional observers can subscribe or unsubscribe at runtime.
  - o Flexible, supports event-driven architecture.
- **Disadvantages**:
  - o Notification can be frequent or inefficient if changes happen often or if many observers are unneeded.
  - o Observers must handle possible concurrency issues or out-of-order updates.

4.8.5 Real-World Examples

- **Event listeners** in GUIs and frameworks like Java's Swing or JavaScript's DOM events.
- **Publish/Subscribe** systems in messaging brokers (e.g., RabbitMQ, Kafka).
- **Data binding** in frameworks like Angular or React (though the implementation details differ, the concept is reminiscent of Observer).

4.9 State Pattern

The **State** pattern allows an object to change its **behavior** when its internal state changes, appearing to the client as if its class has changed. Instead of having large conditionals to check the object's mode or status, each state is represented as a separate class implementing the same interface.

4.9.1 Context and Motivation

Consider a **TCP connection** object with states like **Closed, Listening, Established**. The actions it can perform (open, close, send data) differ by state. Without the State pattern, you might have a massive switch or if-else structure in each method. By representing each state as a class, the context simply delegates to the current state object to handle requests.

4.9.2 Structure and Participants

1. **Context**: Maintains a reference to a State object, which handles requests.
2. **State**: An interface that declares state-specific behavior methods.
3. **ConcreteState**: Implements behavior associated with a particular state. May trigger state transitions.

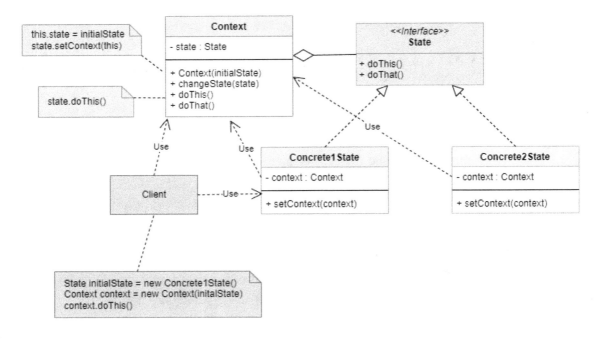

4.9.3 Implementation Details

- **Context Delegation**: The context's methods often simply delegate the call to the current state.
- **Self-Transition**: A state can decide to stay in the same state or switch to a different one.
- **Identifying State Classes**: Each discrete mode or condition of the system becomes a separate class.

Example (Pseudo-Code)

```
interface State {
    void handleRequest(Context context);
}

class Context {
    private State state;
    public Context(State s) {
        this.state = s;
    }
    public void setState(State s) {
        this.state = s;
    }
    public void request() {
        state.handleRequest(this);
```

```
    }
  }

// Concrete states
class ConcreteStateA implements State {
  @Override
  public void handleRequest(Context context) {
    System.out.println("State A handling request. Transitioning to B.");
    context.setState(new ConcreteStateB());
  }
}

class ConcreteStateB implements State {
  @Override
  public void handleRequest(Context context) {
    System.out.println("State B handling request. Transitioning to A.");
    context.setState(new ConcreteStateA());
  }
}

// Usage
class StateDemo {
  public static void main(String[] args) {
    Context c = new Context(new ConcreteStateA());
    c.request(); // handled by A, transitions to B
    c.request(); // handled by B, transitions to A
  }
}
```

4.9.4 Advantages and Disadvantages

- **Advantages**:
  - Eliminates complex conditional logic scattered through the context.
  - Each state is a standalone class, making it easier to add or modify states.
  - Encourages single-responsibility: state-specific behavior lives in the corresponding state class.
- **Disadvantages**:
  - More classes to manage, one per possible state.
  - Transitions can become unclear if not well-documented, leading to confusion

about which states lead to which.

4.9.5 Real-World Examples

- **UI components** that have states like hovered, focused, disabled, pressed.
- **Networking protocols** with states for connecting, disconnecting, transferring data, etc.
- **Game AI**: NPCs can have states like Idle, Patrol, Attack, Flee, each with distinct behavior.

4.10 Strategy Pattern

Strategy defines a family of algorithms, encapsulates each one, and makes them interchangeable at runtime. The client can vary the algorithm used without altering the code that uses the algorithm. This pattern is especially useful when you have different approaches to the same problem—like sorting or calculating routes—that you want to swap easily.

4.10.1 Context and Motivation

Consider an application that sorts data. Sometimes you might prefer **quick sort** for average performance, other times a **merge sort** for stable sorting, or a **heap sort** for certain memory constraints. The Strategy pattern enables these algorithms to be encapsulated in classes implementing a common interface. The client can choose which strategy to apply at runtime based on data characteristics or user preference.

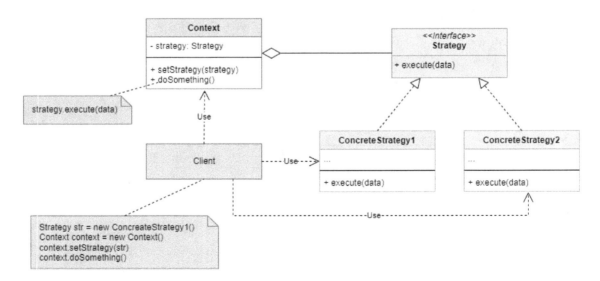

4.10.2 Structure and Participants

1. **Strategy**: Declares the interface for an algorithm.
2. **ConcreteStrategy**: Implements a specific variant of the algorithm.

3. **Context**: Maintains a reference to a Strategy. The client sets or changes the strategy; the context calls doAlgorithm() when needed.

4.10.3 Implementation Details

- **Choosing a Strategy**: Often done by the client. Alternatively, the context itself might decide based on environment or data.
- **Avoiding Conditionals**: By placing different behaviors in different strategies, you remove the need for big conditionals in the context.
- **Data Sharing**: The context might pass data to the strategy or store shared data. The strategy should generally only focus on the algorithmic part.

Example (Pseudo-Code)

```
interface SortingStrategy {
    void sort(List<Integer> data);
}

class QuickSortStrategy implements SortingStrategy {
    @Override
    public void sort(List<Integer> data) {
        // quicksort logic
        System.out.println("Sorting data using QuickSort");
    }
}

class MergeSortStrategy implements SortingStrategy {
    @Override
    public void sort(List<Integer> data) {
        // mergesort logic
        System.out.println("Sorting data using MergeSort");
    }
}

// Context
class DataSet {
    private SortingStrategy strategy;
    private List<Integer> data;

    public DataSet(List<Integer> data) {
```

```
      this.data = data;
    }
    public void setStrategy(SortingStrategy s) {
      this.strategy = s;
    }
    public void sortData() {
      strategy.sort(this.data);
    }
}

// Usage
class StrategyDemo {
    public static void main(String[] args) {
      DataSet ds = new DataSet(Arrays.asList(5,2,7,1));
      ds.setStrategy(new QuickSortStrategy());
      ds.sortData();

      ds.setStrategy(new MergeSortStrategy());
      ds.sortData();
    }
}
```

4.10.4 Advantages and Disadvantages

- **Advantages**:
    - o Simplifies code by removing conditionals for multiple algorithm variations.
    - o Strategies can be swapped out or extended easily.
    - o Promotes single responsibility: each strategy is self-contained.
- **Disadvantages**:
    - o Overhead of creating and using multiple strategy objects.
    - o If data is trivial or the algorithm seldom changes, it may be overkill.

4.10.5 Real-World Examples

- **Various sort or search algorithms** in a library.
- **Route-finding** in navigation apps with different algorithms (fastest route, scenic route, toll avoidance).
- **Compression/Encryption** strategies in file handling.

4.11 Template Method Pattern

Template Method defines the skeleton of an algorithm in a base class, allowing subclasses to **override certain steps** without changing the overall algorithm structure. This pattern ensures consistent high-level flow while letting details vary in specific implementations.

4.11.1 Context and Motivation

When you have an algorithm with a fixed structure or sequence of steps, but some steps can change depending on the scenario, Template Method is a clean solution. For example, a data processing pipeline might always:

1. Read data
2. Parse data
3. Process data
4. Write results

Yet each step can vary across different data sources, formats, or processing logic. The Template Method in the abstract class ensures the sequence remains the same while letting subclasses implement the varying steps.

4.11.2 Structure and Participants

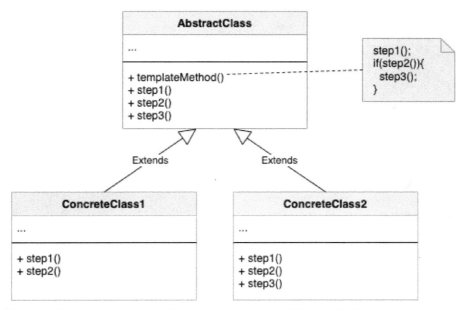

1. **AbstractClass**: Implements the **template method** that calls abstract or hook methods in a certain order.
2. **ConcreteClass**: Overrides the abstract methods or hooks to provide specific behavior. The structure of the algorithm remains in the abstract class.

4.11.3 Implementation Details

- **Template Method**: Typically final in languages that support it, so subclasses cannot override the algorithm's structure.
- **Hooks**: Optional methods that do nothing by default but can be overridden in subclasses for additional customization.
- **Enforced Sequence**: The abstract class ensures the method calls occur in the intended sequence.

Example (Pseudo-Code)

```
abstract class DataProcessor {
    // Template method
    public final void process() {
        readData();
        parseData();
        processData();
        writeResults();
    }

    // Steps to be overridden
    protected abstract void readData();
    protected abstract void parseData();
    protected abstract void processData();

    // Concrete method
    protected void writeResults() {
        System.out.println("Writing results to default location.");
    }
}

// Concrete classes
class CSVDataProcessor extends DataProcessor {
    @Override
    protected void readData() {
        System.out.println("Reading CSV file...");
    }
    @Override
    protected void parseData() {
        System.out.println("Parsing CSV data...");
```

```java
    }
    @Override
    protected void processData() {
        System.out.println("Analyzing parsed CSV data...");
    }
}


class XMLDataProcessor extends DataProcessor {
    @Override
    protected void readData() {
        System.out.println("Reading XML file...");
    }
    @Override
    protected void parseData() {
        System.out.println("Parsing XML data...");
    }
    @Override
    protected void processData() {
        System.out.println("Transforming parsed XML data...");
    }
}


// Usage
class TemplateMethodDemo {
    public static void main(String[] args) {
        DataProcessor csvProcessor = new CSVDataProcessor();
        csvProcessor.process();

        DataProcessor xmlProcessor = new XMLDataProcessor();
        xmlProcessor.process();
    }
}
```

4.11.4 Advantages and Disadvantages

- **Advantages**:
    - o Enforces a standard algorithm structure while allowing variation in details.
    - o Reduces code duplication by placing common steps in the abstract class.
    - o Easy to create new variations by subclassing and overriding specific steps.

- **Disadvantages**:
  - o Requires inheritance, so it might not work as well when using composition-based designs.
  - o Changes to the base class can break subclasses if not done carefully.

4.11.5 Real-World Examples

- **Application frameworks**: The framework calls hook methods in your subclasses.
- **Game development**: A game loop that calls methods for updating, checking collisions, and rendering.
- **Automated testing frameworks**: Setup, test steps, and teardown follow a template method approach.

4.12 Visitor Pattern

The **Visitor** pattern separates an algorithm from the object structure on which it operates, allowing you to add **new operations** to existing object structures without modifying the classes of those structures. This is achieved by letting a visitor **traverse** the structure and call specific methods for each type of element.

4.12.1 Context and Motivation

Sometimes you need to perform varied operations on objects that form a composite or inheritance hierarchy—printing, serialization, code analysis, metrics gathering, etc. Typically, you'd either embed these operations in the classes themselves or rely on instanceof checks or double dispatch. The Visitor pattern avoids bloating the original classes with numerous unrelated methods and helps you maintain **double-dispatch** in object-oriented languages that don't inherently support it.

4.12.2 Structure and Participants

1. **Element**: Declares an accept(Visitor v) method.
2. **ConcreteElement**: Implements accept() to call the appropriate visitXYZ(this) on the Visitor.
3. **Visitor**: Declares visitElementA(ConcreteElementA a), visitElementB(ConcreteElementB b), etc.
4. **ConcreteVisitor**: Implements the operations for each element type.

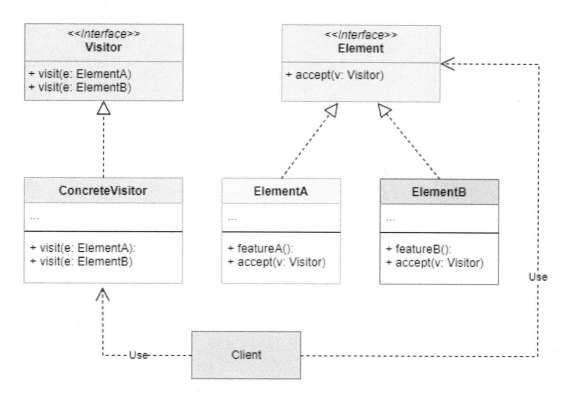

4.12.3 Implementation Details

- **Double Dispatch**: The element calls the visitor's visit method, passing itself as a parameter. This ensures the correct method is invoked based on both the visitor type and the element type.
- **Extending the Algorithm**: To add a new operation, create a new ConcreteVisitor.
- **Extending the Element Hierarchy**: More challenging, as you must update the visitor interface for each new element type.

Example (Pseudo-Code)

```
interface Visitor {
    void visitBook(Book book);
    void visitDVD(DVD dvd);
}

interface ItemElement {
    void accept(Visitor visitor);
}

class Book implements ItemElement {
    private String title;
```

```java
      private int price;
      public Book(String t, int p) { title = t; price = p; }
      public int getPrice() { return price; }
      public String getTitle() { return title; }
      @Override
      public void accept(Visitor visitor) {
         visitor.visitBook(this);
      }
   }

   class DVD implements ItemElement {
      private String name;
      private int price;
      public DVD(String n, int p) { name = n; price = p; }
      public int getPrice() { return price; }
      public String getName() { return name; }
      @Override
      public void accept(Visitor visitor) {
         visitor.visitDVD(this);
      }
   }

   // ConcreteVisitor
   class PriceCalculatorVisitor implements Visitor {
      private int total = 0;
      public void visitBook(Book book) {
         total += book.getPrice();
      }
      public void visitDVD(DVD dvd) {
         total += dvd.getPrice();
      }
      public int getTotal() {
         return total;
      }
   }

   // Usage
   class VisitorDemo {
      public static void main(String[] args) {
```

```
        List<ItemElement> items = Arrays.asList(
            new Book("Design Patterns", 50),
            new DVD("Movie Pack", 30),
            new Book("Clean Code", 40)
        );

        PriceCalculatorVisitor visitor = new PriceCalculatorVisitor();
        for(ItemElement item : items) {
            item.accept(visitor);
        }
        System.out.println("Total cost: " + visitor.getTotal());
    }
}
```

4.12.4 Advantages and Disadvantages

- **Advantages**:
    - o **Open/Closed** principle for new operations: You can add new functionality by adding a visitor rather than changing element classes.
    - o Centralizes operations on a structure in one visitor class.
    - o Avoids repeated instanceof or type checks in the client code.
- **Disadvantages**:
    - o Adding new element types requires updating the Visitor interface (breaking changes).
    - o Requires all elements to have an accept() method, which can be intrusive.
    - o Can lead to a large number of visitor classes if you add many separate operations.

4.12.5 Real-World Examples

- **Abstract syntax trees (ASTs)** in compilers or interpreters, where visitors handle tasks like pretty-printing, optimization, or type checking.
- **XML or JSON parse trees**: Visitors can process, transform, or validate the data.
- **Metrics/gathering** from object models: Each element type has a visitor method to count or analyze attributes.

4.13 Comparing Behavioral Patterns

With the coverage of these 11 main behavioral patterns, let's review how they differ, to assist in selecting the right one for a given scenario:

Pattern	Purpose	Key Distinction
Chain of Responsibility	Pass a request along a chain until one object handles it.	Avoids coupling a sender to a single receiver; each link can handle or pass along.
Command	Encapsulate a request as an object, enabling undo, logging, queuing, etc.	Decouples the invoker from the executor; supports undo/redo and macros.
Interpreter	Define a class-based representation of a language's grammar and interpret sentences in it.	Good for small DSLs or expression parsing; each grammar rule is a class.
Iterator	Provide a way to access the elements of a collection sequentially without exposing internal representation.	Decouples iteration from the collection's data structure.
Mediator	Centralize complex communication among multiple objects, preventing direct references among them.	The mediator orchestrates; colleagues remain decoupled from each other.
Memento	Capture the internal state of an object to restore it later, preserving encapsulation.	Facilitates undo functionality, caretaker stores snapshots without violating encapsulation.
Observer	Define a one-to-many dependency so that observers automatically receive updates from a subject.	Publish-subscribe pattern; flexible, decoupled notifications.
State	Allow an object to alter its behavior when its internal state changes. It appears to change its class.	Eliminate large conditionals by encapsulating state transitions in separate classes.
Strategy	Define a family of algorithms and make them interchangeable.	Encapsulates algorithms in separate classes; the context picks which algorithm to use.

Template Method	Define the skeleton of an algorithm, letting subclasses override certain steps.	Encourages code reuse via inheritance; fixed order with variable steps.
Visitor	Separate operations from the object structure, letting you add new operations without changing the classes.	Uses double-dispatch: each element calls back the visitor's specialized methods.

4.14 Common Pitfalls and Best Practices for Behavioral Patterns

When working with behavioral patterns, keep these pitfalls and guidelines in mind:

1. **Over-Engineering**
   - **Pitfall**: Introducing multiple layers (e.g., a chain or a mediator) when the problem is simple can create needless complexity.
   - **Best Practice**: Evaluate if straightforward solutions (e.g., direct method calls) suffice before adding patterns like Mediator or Chain of Responsibility.

2. **Spaghetti "God" Objects**
   - **Pitfall**: A Mediator or a large set of command classes can become an unmaintainable monolith if it tries to manage everything.
   - **Best Practice**: Keep scope limited. Break up large mediators into smaller domain-specific ones if possible. Keep commands focused on single tasks.

3. **Memory and Performance Overheads**
   - **Pitfall**: Memento and Command patterns can store significant historical or state data.
   - **Best Practice**: Use caching or snapshots judiciously. Clean up old mementos or commands if they no longer matter.

4. **Multiple Observers**
   - **Pitfall**: Observers might cause performance issues or cyclical updates if you're not careful with event ordering or concurrency.
   - **Best Practice**: Design the observer update path so that cycles cannot form or are detected. Optionally throttle or batch notifications for performance.

5. **Maintaining Encapsulation**
   - **Pitfall**: Some patterns (Visitor, Memento) can compromise encapsulation if not carefully designed.
   - **Best Practice**: Use narrow and wide interfaces or protected constructors to ensure external code does not break the object's invariants.

6. **Choosing the Right Pattern**
    o **Pitfall**: Using Strategy when you actually need State logic (or vice versa), or shoehorning a chain when an observer approach might be simpler.
    o **Best Practice**: Distinguish carefully among patterns that appear similar. Patterns like Strategy vs. State or Decorator vs. Proxy (from structural patterns) can cause confusion.

4.15 Real-World Scenarios Integrating Multiple Behavioral Patterns

It's common to see several behavioral patterns working in tandem:

1. **A Text Editor**:
    o **Command** for undo/redo of user operations.
    o **Memento** to store snapshots of editor state for multiple undo levels.
    o **Observer** if multiple views must update when the text changes.
    o **State** for switching between selection mode, insertion mode, or read-only mode.
2. **E-Commerce Ordering System**:
    o **Chain of Responsibility** for handling requests or support tickets.
    o **Observer** for notifying shipping services, payment gateways, or user interfaces about order status changes.
    o **Mediator** if multiple microservices must coordinate but not directly reference each other.
3. **Compiler/Interpreter**:
    o **Interpreter** for parsing smaller expressions or DSL scripts.
    o **Visitor** for traversing the AST to perform semantic checks or code generation.
    o **Memento** might be used for partial rewinding in certain advanced scenarios (less common in compilers, but possible).

By skillfully combining these patterns, developers can craft solutions that are modular, understandable, and robust, even in large-scale systems.

Chapter 5: Design Patterns in Modern Software Development

As software development continues to evolve rapidly—driven by high user expectations, faster release cycles, and sophisticated hardware—a strong foundation in design patterns remains indispensable. While the core ideas of these patterns emerged in an era dominated by desktop and enterprise server applications, they have **adapted** and **expanded** into new domains:

1. **Web development** has grown from serving static pages to delivering large-scale, interactive applications that handle millions of concurrent users.
2. **Mobile development** has emerged as a first-class ecosystem, introducing constraints on performance, battery usage, and connectivity that influence design.
3. **Game development** continually pushes the boundaries of performance and real-time interaction, often requiring specialized architectures that revolve around real-time loops, 2D/3D rendering, and event-driven logic.
4. **Microservices** have revolutionized distributed computing, emphasizing elasticity, fault tolerance, and clear service boundaries in highly decoupled systems.

5.1 Design Patterns in Web Development

Web development is one of the fastest-evolving segments of software engineering. The shift from purely server-rendered pages to **single-page applications (SPAs)** and microservices-based back-ends has required developers to adapt classical design thinking to the demands of stateless protocols, asynchronous operations, and highly interactive user interfaces.

5.1.1 Evolution from Monoliths to Modular Web Architectures

Historically, web applications often followed a **monolithic** pattern, where the server (running frameworks like PHP, Ruby on Rails, or Django) handled everything—from receiving HTTP requests, applying business logic, generating HTML templates, and communicating with databases. Over time, the logic that was once jammed into massive controllers and "God objects" has broken out into well-structured classes and modules, guided by the same design principles and patterns used in desktop applications.

Modern web development typically embraces more **modular** and **distributed** approaches:

- **MVC (Model-View-Controller)** on the server side, occasionally combined with additional patterns on the client side.
- **MVP (Model-View-Presenter)** or **MVVM (Model-View-ViewModel)** in front-end frameworks such as Angular, Vue, React (though React ironically does not explicitly call its approach MVVM, it resembles it in many respects).
- **Service-Oriented** or **microservices** back ends, each service potentially employing specialized patterns to manage data consistency, handle asynchronous events, or maintain domain logic.

5.1.2 Applying Classic Patterns in Web Contexts

Many of the classic design patterns find new life in web development, albeit with a distinctive twist:

- **Adapter** (Client-Side Integrations): Web apps often integrate third-party libraries or APIs that do not match the internal data structures or method signatures. For instance, you might have a payment processing library with a specific function signature, but your front-end code expects a simpler interface. An adapter can seamlessly wrap these external calls.
- **Strategy** (Form Validations or Dynamic Routing): Front-end frameworks might swap in different validation strategies based on the user's locale or data type. On the server side, you might handle different routing strategies for SEO-friendly URLs versus API endpoints.
- **Observer** (Reactive UI Updates): Front-end libraries commonly adopt an observer-like approach to data binding, especially in frameworks that support reactivity. Angular watchers or React's state management reflect observer principles, automatically rerendering components when state changes.
- **Factory** (Resource Creation in APIs): Many web back ends produce resource representations (JSON objects) according to client requests. A factory pattern can handle the "type" of resource a user requests (e.g., user profiles, product details), encapsulating creation logic for each resource shape.

Diagram: Web MVC with Observer Elements

Below is a simplified textual diagram illustrating a server-side MVC approach combined with an observer-like pattern for real-time UI updates. The user interacts with the **Controller**, which updates the **Model**. The model notifies any real-time services or pushes changes to websockets, which in turn update the **View**:

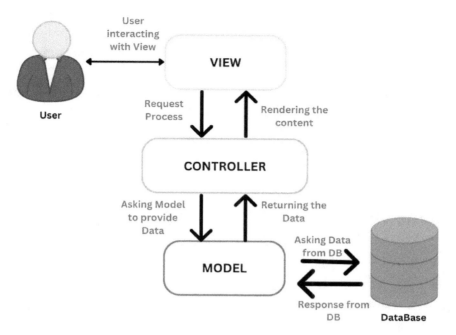

5.1.3 Asynchronous Patterns and Concurrency

A hallmark of web applications is the **asynchronous** nature of operations. The typical user request might spawn multiple asynchronous calls: database queries, microservice requests, caching layers, message queue operations, etc. Patterns such as **Command**, **Mediator**, or **Observer** can be adapted to coordinate these tasks without blocking.

For example, a modern Node.js application might use a **Command**-like approach to queue up tasks for execution, log them, or apply an undo logic in an administrative interface. Meanwhile, **Mediators** coordinate multiple microservices behind the scenes, presenting a unified interface to the front-end.

5.1.4 State Management and Patterns for SPAs

Single-page applications often rely heavily on **client-side state management**. Libraries like **Redux** or **MobX** in the React ecosystem exhibit design patterns akin to **Observer** or **Mediator**:

- **Observer-like**: A Redux store holds the global state, and React components subscribe to slices of that state. Updates automatically re-render components.
- **Strategy** for Reduction: Redux uses "reducers" that apply different strategies for computing new states based on actions.
- **Command** parallels in Redux actions: Each action can be seen as a "command object" describing what changed in the application.

5.1.5 Integration with Cloud and APIs

Modern web apps are rarely self-contained; they integrate with multiple external services, from **cloud storage** to **machine learning** APIs. **Facade** patterns frequently appear here: for instance, a single "PaymentService" facade might aggregate calls to PayPal, Stripe, or custom payment gateways, presenting one unified interface to the rest of the application. Meanwhile, the underlying complexity is encapsulated behind the facade.

Chain of Responsibility can also manifest in API gatekeepers or request-processing pipelines, where each link in the chain adds headers, validates tokens, logs requests, or checks for certain conditions before finally reaching the main business logic.

5.2 Design Patterns in Mobile Application Development

Mobile applications (for iOS, Android, and cross-platform frameworks) contend with performance constraints, battery usage, network variability, and user interface guidelines. Despite these unique pressures, design patterns remain crucial in delivering maintainable code and consistent user experiences.

5.2.1 Dominant Architectural Patterns on Mobile

Mobile platforms commonly leverage architectural patterns like **MVC, MVVM, MVP,** or variations thereof. For example, Apple's iOS once advocated MVC as exemplified by **UIKit** structures, but the community has widely adopted or adapted **MVVM** with frameworks such as RxSwift or Combine to handle reactive data flows.

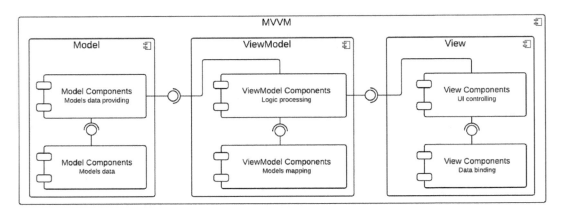

On Android, the official guidelines have evolved from the somewhat "God Activity" approach to **MVP** or **MVVM** with **LiveData, ViewModel,** and **Data Binding** libraries. These architectures help separate concerns: the UI or "View" layer is minimal and binds to a "ViewModel" that implements business logic. Observers or reactive streams notify the view of changes.

5.2.2 Adapting Classic Patterns to Mobile Constraints

While the base patterns remain the same, the constraints of mobile drive their usage:

- **Singleton** for Central Services: Because mobile devices have limited memory, a single instance approach is often used for central resources such as location services, analytics trackers, or database managers. However, developers must be cautious with memory usage and potential concurrency issues.

- **Decorator** for UI Components: In some UI frameworks, adding features like border, shadows, or special behaviors to a basic view can be done with decorator-like wrappers or specialized layout containers.

- **Adapter** for Data Binding: Many mobile UIs revolve around "adapters" in a sense reminiscent of the pattern name. For instance, in Android, you have ListAdapter or RecyclerView.Adapter, bridging data sets to display elements.

-

Diagram: MVVM in a Mobile App

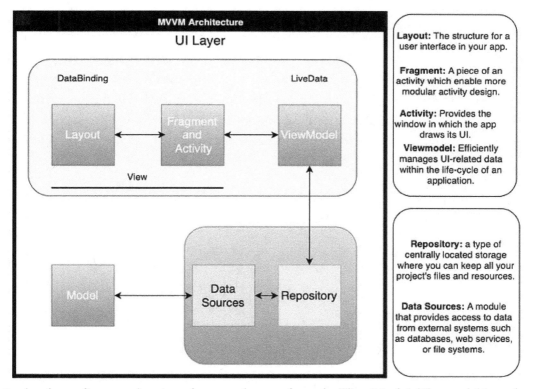

In the above diagram, the view observes changes from the **ViewModel**. The model is updated independently, often through repository patterns or direct data access. This fosters a decoupled architecture suitable for testability and reusability.

5.2.3 Offline Capabilities and State Synchronization

Mobile apps must handle intermittent connectivity. Patterns can help:

- **Memento**-like strategies for saving local state.
- **Observer** or **Publisher-Subscriber** approaches for synchronizing local changes with the server once connectivity is restored.
- **Facade** for abstracting offline/online differences, letting the rest of the app remain agnostic to whether the user is connected.

5.2.4 Performance and Battery Optimization

Because battery life is a premium on mobile devices, unnecessary processing or complicated object relationships can degrade performance. Many developers rely on **Flyweight**-style approaches for caching and reusing UI elements, images, or data sets. This helps limit memory usage and CPU cycles, particularly in list or grid-based UIs that display repetitive items.

Similarly, the **Strategy** pattern can help dynamically choose the best approach for a given network condition—e.g., a "HighQualityStrategy" for images when on Wi-Fi, versus a "LowBandwidthStrategy" on cellular data.

5.2.5 Cross-Platform Frameworks and Patterns

Tools like **Flutter**, **React Native**, or **Xamarin** unify the mobile codebase across platforms but still encourage design patterns. React Native fosters a strongly reactive environment reminiscent of observer patterns, while Flutter's approach to widgets involves composition that can recall patterns like **Decorator** and **Builder**. The underlying principles remain the same: separate concerns, keep data flows clear, and ensure robust resource management.

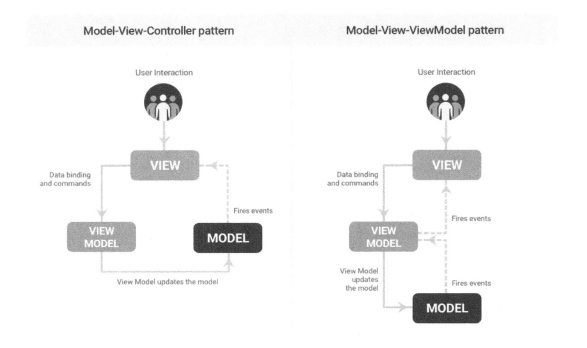

5.3 Design Patterns in Game Development

Game development is a world of real-time rendering, user input processing, and constantly changing states. Although many classic patterns remain relevant, the domain has also inspired specialized variations or unique uses.

5.3.1 Game Loops and Real-Time Constraints

Most games revolve around a **game loop** that runs many times per second, updating game state, processing input, and rendering graphics. While not a design pattern in the traditional sense, the loop structure interacts with patterns such as:

- **Observer**: Entities in the game that watch for events like collisions, player input, or triggers.
- **Mediator**: Coordinating different subsystems (physics, AI, rendering) so they don't become tightly coupled.
- **State**: Representing different modes an entity or the overall game can be in (Paused, Running, Game Over, etc.).

5.3.2 Entity-Component-System (ECS)

One popular architecture in modern game engines is **Entity-Component-System** (ECS). Although not originally described in the Gang of Four patterns, ECS aligns well with design principles that emphasize composition over inheritance.

- **Entities** are essentially IDs or containers.
- **Components** hold data or small behaviors (e.g., position, sprite, collision shape).
- **Systems** process sets of entities that have the necessary components.

An ECS approach often uses patterns like **Observer** to notify systems of changes, or **Factory** to instantiate new entities with certain components attached. ECS is prized for its performance (cache-friendly data layout) and flexible composition of behaviors.

5.3.3 Behavioral Patterns for NPCs and AI

Behavioral patterns like **Strategy** or **State** figure prominently in AI logic:

- **Strategy**: Different AI behaviors or pathfinding algorithms (e.g., A*, BFS, steering behaviors) can be swapped depending on the game scenario or difficulty level.
- **State**: Non-player characters (NPCs) often revolve among states (Patrolling, Chasing, Attacking, Fleeing). Each state is encapsulated in a separate class to avoid monstrous switch statements.

Command is also used in multi-step sequences—particularly for **scripting** or controlling cutscenes. A sequence of commands can be queued to animate characters or trigger in-game events.

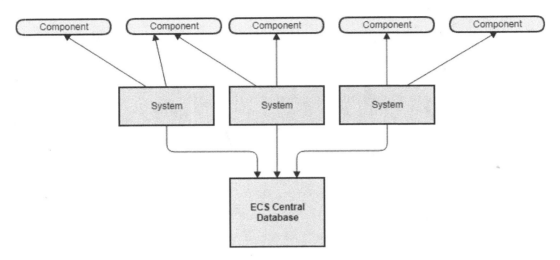

Systems operate on sets of Entities that have the needed Components.

5.3.4 Resource Management and Optimization

Games must manage large assets: textures, models, sounds, etc. Patterns help:

- **Singleton** or **Service Locator** to retrieve shared resources such as a texture cache or audio engine.
- **Flyweight** for reusing mesh data across many instances of the same model or repeating texture tiles.
- **Prototype** in level editors or game creation tools, letting designers clone "prototype" enemies or items.

5.3.5 Networking and Multiplayer

When building online or multiplayer games, patterns such as **Proxy** and **Observer** become crucial. A **remote proxy** might represent remote players or a remote game server. Observers watch for network messages (e.g., move commands, chat messages) and then update local game state accordingly.

Additionally, **Chain of Responsibility** can handle input events in a local environment. Key presses or gamepad events might pass through multiple layers—UI, debugging overlays, the game logic itself—until something handles them.

5.4 Microservices and Design Patterns

The rise of **microservices** has transformed how large-scale systems are built and deployed.

Instead of a single monolithic deployment, functionality is decomposed into many smaller, autonomous services. Each microservice is responsible for a specific domain or bounded context, communicates over the network (often via REST, gRPC, or messaging), and can scale independently. Classical design patterns remain relevant inside each service, but the distributed nature of microservices also introduces new patterns and considerations at the architectural level.

5.4.1 Distinguishing Microservices Patterns

While the **Gang of Four** patterns primarily focus on object-oriented design, microservices patterns address higher-level architectural concerns:

- **Service Discovery**: Mechanisms like **Consul** or **Eureka** locate services at runtime.
- **API Gateway** or **BFF (Backend for Frontend)**: Functions as a **Facade** pattern at the system level, providing a simplified interface to many backend services.
- **Saga**: A pattern to manage distributed transactions across multiple microservices.
- **Circuit Breaker**: A resilience pattern that acts somewhat like a **Proxy**, short-circuiting calls to an unresponsive or failing service.

Although these are distinct from the original design patterns, they share the same spirit: **enhancing maintainability, reliability, and clarity** through standardized solutions for recurring distributed problems.

5.4.2 Applying Classic Patterns in Microservices

Within each microservice, classical patterns remain valuable:

- **Repository** or **Data Mapper** patterns for persisting domain objects (these are domain-driven design patterns, but they have synergy with the same problem/solution thinking of design patterns).
- **Factory** or **Builder** for creating complex domain entities.
- **Observer** or **Publisher-Subscriber** for decoupled event-driven communication. This often aligns with the use of message brokers like RabbitMQ or Kafka, where one service publishes an event, and multiple others subscribe.
- **Strategy** for choosing different business logic pathways (e.g., shipping methods, discount calculations) within the microservice.

5.4.3 Resilience and Communication Patterns

Due to network unpredictability, microservices rely on patterns that handle **partial failures** gracefully:

- **Circuit Breaker**: Monitors calls to a remote service. If calls fail repeatedly, the breaker "opens," preventing further requests for a cooldown period. Conceptually, it acts like a specialized proxy or "guard" object that intercepts calls.
- **Retry and Backoff**: A simple pattern to re-attempt requests. Could be implemented with

a **Decorator** pattern around the client code, automatically retrying on failure.

- **Bulkhead**: Partition resources (threads, memory) to avoid a failing service from cascading to others, reminiscent of a containment approach.

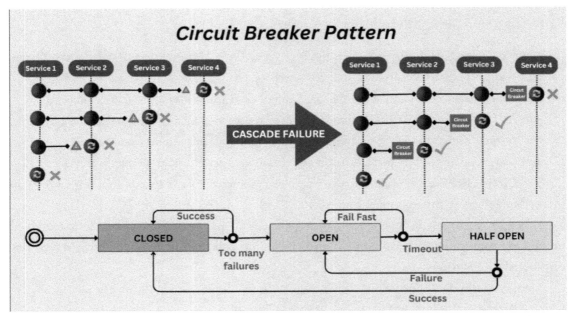

The API Gateway or a specialized library can wrap calls in circuit breakers, which if open, immediately return a fallback or error response without hitting the failing service.

5.4.4 Data Consistency Patterns

Microservices often maintain separate databases. Ensuring eventual consistency requires patterns that coordinate data changes:

- **Saga** for distributed transactions: A series of local transactions across multiple services. If one step fails, compensating actions roll back the previous steps.
- **Outbox** or **Transaction Log Tailing** approach: The service writes events or changes to an outbox table, read by a background process that publishes them to a message broker. This fosters an **Observer**-like event flow without directly coupling services.

5.4.5 Domain-Driven Design (DDD) Synergy

Microservices commonly pair with Domain-Driven Design. DDD is not a "design pattern" library per se, but it does introduce concepts like **Aggregates**, **Entities**, **Value Objects**, and **Repositories** that complement the classic design patterns. The synergy is strong:

- **Entities** can apply patterns like **State** internally if they have multiple states (e.g., an Order with states: Created, Paid, Shipped).

- **Repositories** often incorporate **Factory** or **Builder** logic to reconstitute aggregates from persistence.
- **Domain Events** align with an **Observer** or "publish-subscribe" style, triggered inside a microservice's domain layer to notify others of changes.

Chapter 6: Anti-Patterns and Common Pitfalls

The term **anti-pattern** was popularized to describe repeated, tempting, but ultimately harmful design or organizational decisions in software development. These mistakes often arise due to time pressure, lack of clear architecture, or misguided attempts to quickly solve problems. Over time, certain negative practices have shown up repeatedly across projects of all sizes and in all languages, which is why they have been catalogued and named—allowing us to share cautionary tales and prevention strategies.

6.1 Defining Anti-Patterns

An **anti-pattern** is best thought of as a commonly repeated solution to a recurring problem that yields **negative consequences** over time. It is not simply "bad code" or "bad design"—rather, it is a *recognized* misguided approach that arises due to lack of clarity, communication, or design foresight. Much like a design pattern describes a best practice for a known scenario, an anti-pattern outlines a **worst practice**—something that is often chosen due to convenience or familiarity but is ultimately detrimental.

Common characteristics of an anti-pattern include:

- **Recurrence**: The same structural or behavioral flaws appear across many projects.
- **Initial Appeal**: On the surface, the approach might seem convenient, easy, or even intuitive.
- **Negative Impact**: Over time, maintainability, performance, scalability, or correctness significantly degrade.
- **Refactor-Ability**: In many cases, anti-patterns can be refactored away by introducing correct design patterns or improved architectural decisions.

By systematically studying anti-patterns, teams gain a **shared vocabulary** for identifying problematic code structures and can unify around the necessity of refactoring or redesign. These "red flags" in a code review or design discussion can trigger immediate recognition: "This is turning into a God Object scenario, we should break it up," or "We're inadvertently building a new Inner Platform, let's pivot to simpler solutions." Catching anti-patterns early prevents them from becoming entrenched, saving significant effort down the line.

6.2 God Object

Among the most notorious anti-patterns is the **God Object**, which arises when a single class or component accumulates **too many responsibilities** or too much domain knowledge. This class effectively becomes the "center of the universe," dealing with too many tasks—often because developers keep adding more logic to it over time, rather than creating new classes or modules.

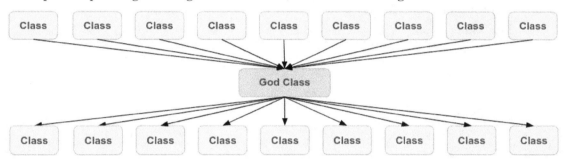

6.2.1 Symptoms and Impact

God objects often manifest in these ways:
- **Massive Lines of Code**: The file might balloon to thousands of lines.
- **Excessive Coupling**: Most other classes in the system import or reference this "God Class."
- **Constructor or Method Bloat**: The class might have a large number of methods, or a constructor with many parameters.
- **Inconsistent Responsibilities**: The same class handles data validation, network calls, data storage, and application logic, all in one place.

The effects on the codebase are pernicious:
- **Code Instability**: Any change in the God Object risks breaking seemingly unrelated parts of the system.
- **Difficult Testing**: A test suite for that class might require extensive mocks and stubs, or else testers skip rigorous tests altogether.

- **Hard-to-Understand Code**: New developers must spend excessive time deciphering how the God Object works, delaying onboarding and feature development.

6.2.2 Causes

A God Object typically arises from repeated small design shortcuts. For instance, a developer might decide, "I'll add this small feature to the main controller since it's already partially relevant," or "We can't bother with a new class now; we'll just put the logic in X for speed." Over time, these "quick fixes" accumulate into an unmanageable behemoth.

6.2.3 Refactoring / Prevention

- **Refactor to Smaller Classes**: Identify natural boundaries (e.g., feature sets, domains), then **extract classes** or modules for each boundary.
- **Apply Single Responsibility Principle**: Ensure each class or module addresses one primary concern.
- **Introduce Layers**: If the God Object commingles data access, business logic, and UI, separate them into distinct layers (following MVC or similar).
- **Continuous Code Reviews**: Peer reviews should watch for newly introduced methods that do not fit the class's core responsibility.

6.2.4 Diagram Example

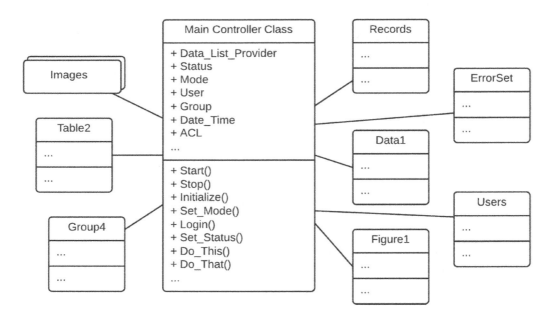

In this depiction, nearly every other part of the system references or depends on MainController, making it an obvious "God Object."

6.3 Singleton Overuse

While **Singleton** (discussed in earlier chapters as a design pattern) can be valid in limited contexts where you truly need **exactly one** instance of a class (e.g., a global logging facility), **Singleton Overuse** arises when developers designate classes as singletons for convenience, rather than necessity. This leads to hidden dependencies, global state, and testability issues.

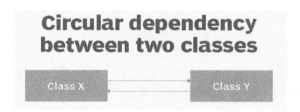

6.3.1 Why It Becomes an Anti-Pattern

Singleton can morph from a beneficial pattern into an anti-pattern when:
1. **Global State Proliferates**: Many singletons create widely shared data that can change unpredictably, making it hard to track or debug.
2. **Test Barriers**: Because singletons are globally accessible, writing unit tests that require different instance configurations or mocking becomes complicated.
3. **Tight Coupling**: Code all over the system references singletons directly, leading to a spiderweb of dependencies that hamper refactoring.

6.3.2 Indicators of Overuse

- **Multiple Singletons** for logically separate concerns. A system with 8 or 9 singletons likely signals design missteps.
- **Eager Instantiation** even when the service is rarely used, wasting resources.
- **Difficult Mocks**: You find yourself writing hacky solutions to mock or reset singletons for test runs.

6.3.3 Migration Strategies

- **Replace Singleton with a Dependency Injection** approach, so you can control the lifecycle and number of instances as needed.
- **Use Named Instances**: If your reason for singletons was "only one instance," but occasionally you need multiple, revert to a normal class with named or limited instances.
- **Inversion of Control (IoC)**: Rely on frameworks or factories to create and manage the object, removing direct dependencies on global singletons.

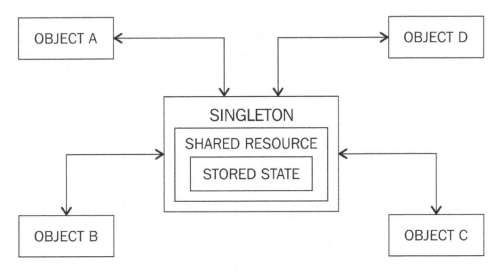

Every part of the system references multiple singletons, creating a web of global state.

6.4 Circular Dependencies

A **circular dependency** occurs when two or more modules or classes indirectly depend on each other. For instance, Class A depends on Class B, which depends on Class C, which depends on Class A. This is often subtle—some references might be hidden behind aggregator classes or indirect calls. Nonetheless, circular dependencies can hamper maintainability and lead to issues such as **compilation errors** in certain languages, **initialization order** problems, or **runtime crashes**.

6.4.1 Symptoms

- **Initialization Hell**: Two components that rely on each other's constructors, causing indefinite or partial initialization states.
- **Hidden Coupling**: Breaking any of the involved classes leads to cascading changes or refactoring headaches.
- **Complex Build Processes**: Some languages (like Java, .NET) can handle forward references, but cyclical references in complex frameworks or C++ can cause linking issues or require unnatural code arrangement.

6.4.2 Example Scenario

A simplistic example in pseudo-code:

```
class ClassA {
    private ClassB b;
```

```
    public ClassA() {
        b = new ClassB(); // But ClassB also needs ClassA
    }
}

class ClassB {
    private ClassA a;
    public ClassB() {
        a = new ClassA(); // leads to infinite recursion or partial init
    }
}
```

While obviously contrived, real-world cycles often appear in large codebases with multiple classes referencing each other through a chain. For example, UserService depends on OrderService, which references PaymentService, which calls back into UserService.

6.4.3 Solving and Preventing Circular Dependencies

- **Decouple with Interfaces**: Insert an interface boundary or abstract base class to break direct references.
- **Refactor Common Logic**: If two classes keep referencing each other's functionality, consider extracting the overlapping logic into a third module that each can import.
- **Avoid Overly Large Modules**: In languages with module-level imports, be mindful of how you group classes. Splitting them into more coherent modules can reduce cyclical references.

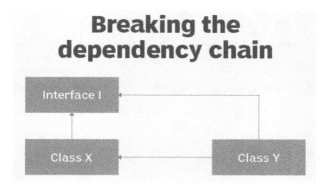

6.5 Hard-Coded Dependencies

When a class explicitly **creates or configures** the objects it relies on—rather than receiving them via constructor parameters, factories, or dependency injection—we call this a **hard-coded dependency**. This practice reduces flexibility and testability.

6.5.1 Consequences

- **Difficult Unit Testing**: If a class unconditionally instantiates a concrete FileLogger, you cannot easily substitute a MockLogger.
- **Reduced Reusability**: You cannot reuse the code in contexts where a different resource or service is required.
- **Hidden Coupling**: The code references concrete types everywhere, instead of more abstract interfaces.

6.5.2 Example

```
class PaymentProcessor {
    private BankAPI bank;
    public PaymentProcessor() {
        // Hard-coded dependency to external BankAPI
        this.bank = new BankAPI("mySecretKey");
    }
    // ...
}
```

6.5.3 Solutions

- **Dependency Injection** (constructor or setter injection): Let external code pass in an interface or a prebuilt object.
- **Service Locators**: Some contexts use a centralized registry, though that can be an anti-pattern if misused.
- **Factory or Abstract Factory**: For creation logic that absolutely must occur within the class, hide it behind a more flexible abstraction.

6.6 Spaghetti Code

"Spaghetti Code" is a colloquial term for software that has **little to no discernible structure**, with **control flow** that jumps around unpredictably (like entangled noodles). Though not always recognized as a formal "anti-pattern," it is widely acknowledged as one of the worst states for code.

6.6.1 Characteristics

- **No Clear Modules or Layers**: Logic is scattered or repeated across the codebase, with no separation of concerns.
- **Long, Tangled Methods**: A single method might handle everything from user input to data storage.
- **High Complexity**: Cyclomatic complexity is often extremely high—lots of nested loops or conditionals.

6.6.2 Why It Emerges

Spaghetti code typically results from:

- **Incremental, Unplanned Growth**: Feature after feature added to existing routines.
- **No Code Reviews**: A lack of accountability or oversight.
- **Excessive Urgency**: "We'll just hack this in for the deadline," repeated many times.

6.6.3 Refactoring Approaches

- **Identify and Extract** cohesive blocks into new functions or classes.
- **Write Unit Tests** around existing code to ensure refactoring does not break functionality.
- **Introduce Patterns**: Where you see repeated logic or tangles, consider a recognized design pattern to structure the solution.

6.7 Golden Hammer

The **Golden Hammer** is a conceptual anti-pattern where a team or developer "**loves**" a specific technology, pattern, or approach so much that they apply it to every problem, whether it fits or not. The name references the adage: "If all you have is a hammer, everything looks like a nail."

6.7.1 Examples

1. A developer enamored with microservices breaks an application into dozens of tiny services, despite minimal need for that complexity.
2. Using a full-blown event-sourcing approach for small, straightforward CRUD operations.
3. Implementing an **Observer** pattern for a single event with one subscriber, where a direct function call would suffice.

6.7.2 Negative Outcomes

- **Overcomplication**: The solution becomes more complex, with more overhead than necessary.

- **Inflexibility**: Because the same pattern or library is forced onto new problems, domain-specific solutions can't be explored.
- **Wasted Time**: Staff invests time learning or managing an elaborate approach for trivial tasks.

6.7.3 Mitigation

- **Evaluate Use Cases**: For each new problem, consider alternate approaches.
- **Prototype** or do a small proof-of-concept to see if the pattern or library is a good fit.
- **Diverse Tooling**: Encourage the team to master multiple design patterns and frameworks, not just one "golden" approach.

6.8 Lava Flow

"Lava Flow" refers to **dead or inert code** that remains in a system because nobody dares or bothers to remove it. It is akin to hardened lava that once flowed actively but now sits, immovable, in the codebase. Over time, as the original reason for that code fades from collective memory, the code remains, adding confusion and complexity.

6.8.1 Why Lava Flow Occurs

- **Fear**: Removing the code might break something unknown, so the team leaves it in place.
- **Poor Documentation**: The code's purpose is unclear, so it's safer to keep it than to risk deleting it.
- **Lack of Ownership**: The original authors are gone, and no one wants the responsibility of removing or refactoring mysterious logic.

6.8.2 Consequences

- **Bloated Codebase**: Maintenance overhead grows as developers must sift through code that might be non-functional.
- **Potential for Unexpected Behavior**: If accidentally invoked, the old code might conflict with newer logic.
- **Obfuscation**: Undocumented, unused classes or modules create confusion for new developers.

6.8.3 Remedies

- **Code Audits**: Systematically identify classes or functions that are never called.
- **Use Feature Flags** or environment toggles to test removing certain chunks.

- **Maintain Good Documentation**: Keep track of reasons for code, or remove it promptly when obsolete.

6.9 Poltergeist

A **Poltergeist** class or object is one that **appears briefly**, possibly just to pass data from one method to another, and then disappears. It provides minimal or no real functionality. This ephemeral presence is typically a sign of a design that can be simplified—these classes add an extra layer of indirection without real value.

6.9.1 Indicators

- A class is used in only one place, for a trivial wrapper around some data or a single method call.
- The object's constructor or destructor do essentially nothing, and the class holds no state.
- Removal of the poltergeist class and direct integration into the calling code yields no negative side effects.

6.9.2 Reasons for Poltergeist Classes

- **Over-Engineering**: The developer might be trying to follow some pattern blindly (e.g., "everything must be an object"), leading to unneeded classes.
- **Past Plans**: The class might have been intended to do more, but that logic never materialized.

6.9.3 Solutions

- **Inline or Merge** the poltergeist into the calling code or a more relevant class.
- **Refocus on Single Responsibility**: If the ephemeral class is truly needed, clarify its unique responsibility; otherwise remove it.

6.10 Cut-and-Paste / Copy-Pasta Programming

A ubiquitous pitfall is **duplicate code** introduced by copying and pasting from one part of the codebase to another. While it might save time initially, it undermines maintainability because **fixes or enhancements** must be repeated across all duplicates.

6.10.1 Symptoms

- **Identical Code Blocks** in multiple files, possibly with only small naming changes.

- **Inconsistent Bug Fixes**: One copy is patched, while others remain broken.
- **Code Bloat**: The codebase swells with repeated logic.

6.10.2 Why It Happens

- **Time Pressure**: Copy-paste is seen as the fastest approach.
- **Poor Abstractions**: The system lacks a well-designed function, class, or module to share that logic.
- **Example Reliance**: Developers may copy official or community code examples verbatim, never refactoring them for their specific usage.

6.10.3 Best Practices

- **Extract Common Functions** or classes for any code that must appear in more than one place.
- **Review for Duplication**: Code review or static analysis tools can detect suspiciously similar blocks.
- **Encourage Reuse**: Maintain a library or utility module for shared behaviors.

6.11 Premature Optimization

Premature optimization arises when developers focus on micro-level performance tweaks before verifying the need through profiling or actual user metrics. While optimizing code is beneficial, doing so **too early** can lead to architectural distortions or overcomplicated solutions for minimal real-world gains.

6.11.1 Negative Results

- **Complex, Hard-to-Read Code**: Data structures or algorithms chosen purely for theoretical speed might complicate everything else.
- **Wasted Effort**: The performance bottleneck might lie elsewhere, like I/O or network latency.
- **Inflexible Architecture**: Over-optimized code can hamper future feature additions or expansions.

6.11.2 Strategies to Avoid It

- **Profile First**: Gather actual runtime data to identify top bottlenecks.
- **Implement a Baseline**: Start with a clean, maintainable design and optimize the critical paths once they are proven to be slow.

- **Document Rationale**: If you do optimize early, record your justification and the measured performance impact.

6.12 Inner-Platform Effect

The **Inner-Platform Effect** refers to designing a system that attempts to mimic or recreate **capabilities already provided** by the programming platform, language, or framework. This often leads to an over-engineered environment that basically replicates the features of the underlying environment in a more cumbersome way.

6.12.1 Manifestations

- Building a custom "object model" on top of an OOP language, re-implementing things like inheritance or virtual dispatch.
- Creating a "scripting engine" that essentially replicates the language's own runtime or library features in a less efficient manner.
- Designing elaborate frameworks for tasks that a simpler or standard library solution would handle elegantly.

6.12.2 Why This Happens

- **Mistrust or Lack of Knowledge**: Developers might not be fully aware of built-in features or standard libraries.
- **Desire for Control**: A misguided sense that re-implementing everything in-house grants more reliability or customization.
- **Hubris**: Overconfidence in "doing it better" than the established tools.

6.12.3 Avoidance

- **Leverage Standard Libraries**: Before writing custom frameworks, research existing solutions or official libraries.
- **Keep It Simple**: Use the language features as designed unless you have a very specific, justified reason to deviate.
- **Periodic Architectural Audits**: Check if new functionalities are duplicating the underlying platform's capabilities.

6.13 Bicycle Shed (Parkinson's Law of Triviality)

Though somewhat more organizational than purely technical, the **Bicycle Shed** anti-pattern (also known as **Parkinson's Law of Triviality**) describes a scenario in which a team **over-fixates**

on trivial details while neglecting more complex, critical issues. The name comes from an anecdote: a committee can spend hours discussing the color of a bicycle shed (a cheap, low-stakes matter) while breezing past a large nuclear reactor design that is far more complex but less accessible to superficial debate.

6.13.1 Signs of This Anti-Pattern

- **Long Debates Over Minor UI Tweaks** while major architectural decisions remain unaddressed.
- **Committee Bloat**: Many people weigh in on an issue because it's easy to understand or has visible effects, overshadowing deeper design complexities.
- **Lack of Progress** on truly critical tasks because minor decisions consume disproportionate time.

6.13.2 Mitigation Techniques

- **Define Clear Priorities**: Tackle the most impactful features or design choices first, leaving trivial details for later.
- **Empower Experts**: Let domain experts handle complex technical decisions, with a minimum of overhead from novices.
- **Timeboxing**: Limit the discussion time for minor issues so they do not balloon into prolonged controversies.

6.14 Other Common Pitfalls

Beyond the more formally named anti-patterns, a few other pitfalls frequently compromise software projects:

6.14.1 Reinventing the Wheel

Developers sometimes re-implement common functionalities (e.g., caching, authentication, data structures) instead of using **well-tested libraries**. This can waste time, introduce more bugs, and hamper maintainability. Whenever possible, adopting robust, open-source or built-in solutions is more efficient than rolling your own from scratch.

6.14.2 Big-Bang Integration

In large projects, teams might develop multiple modules or components separately, then attempt a massive, last-minute integration. This often results in **integration hell**, with avalanche of conflicting changes, incompatibilities, and undone merges. Continuous integration or smaller incremental merges typically ensure issues are caught early.

6.14.3 Fear of Rewriting

Some teams cling to flawed codebases, reluctant to refactor or rewrite sections that are deeply broken. While rewriting can be risky, ignoring fundamental flaws in the name of "stability" can lead to accumulating technical debt. Judicious partial rewrites or heavy refactoring can pay off if done with proper planning and testing.

6.15 Diagnosing and Correcting Anti-Patterns

The final step in effectively dealing with anti-patterns is learning how to **diagnose** them in real-world code and how to plan a **correction** or **refactoring** strategy. Diagnosis often comes from the synergy of code reviews, static analysis, developer intuition, and testing outcomes.

6.15.1 Steps for Diagnosis

1. **Observation**: Notice repeated complaints from developers or confusion about certain parts of the system.
2. **Identify Patterns**: Compare the problematic code to known anti-pattern definitions.
3. **Measure Impact**: Evaluate how significantly this issue impedes new features, performance, or stability.

6.15.2 Planning a Refactor

- **Scope**: Is the anti-pattern localized (like a single God Class) or pervasive (spaghetti code across the entire system)?
- **Risk Assessment**: Understand dependencies, test coverage, and potential user impact.
- **Incremental vs. All-at-Once**: Evaluate if you can fix it in small steps or if a big rewrite is safer.
- **Communication**: Notify stakeholders about the reason for refactoring, the expected timeline, and potential benefits.

6.15.3 Tools and Techniques

- **Automated Refactoring Tools** in modern IDEs can assist with extracting classes, renaming methods, or removing dead code.
- **Static Analysis** or "lint" tools can detect certain issues, like large classes or repeated code blocks.
- **Continuous Integration** ensures that refactoring merges do not break existing functionality.

Chapter 7: Design Patterns and Software Architecture

Software architecture and design patterns are often viewed as distinct topics, but in reality, they are tightly interwoven. Architecture defines the **macro-level** structure of a software system—its principal components, their responsibilities, and how they interact. Design patterns operate at a more **micro-level**, offering proven solutions to common design problems within those components and interactions. When used effectively, design patterns reinforce the architectural vision, ensuring that large-scale structures remain coherent as teams implement specific features and business logic.

7.1 Layered Architecture and Patterns

One of the most enduring software architecture paradigms is the **layered** (or **tiered**) approach. The underlying principle is that software is organized into horizontal layers, each with a specific set of responsibilities. Classic examples include:

- **Presentation Layer**: Handles user interaction, UI rendering, or front-end logic.
- **Application / Service Layer**: Coordinates business logic, orchestrating use cases and workflows.
- **Domain / Business Layer**: Contains the core domain models and logic that represent the problem space.
- **Infrastructure / Data Access Layer**: Deals with persistence, external systems, file systems, networking, etc.

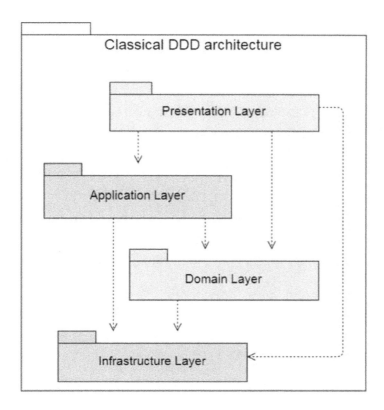

7.1.1 The Rationale for Layered Architecture

A layered approach provides two fundamental benefits:

1. **Separation of Concerns**: Each layer focuses on a narrower aspect of the system, reducing complexity and coupling. This fosters maintainability, as changes in one layer (e.g., database storage optimization) do not ripple uncontrollably through the rest of the code.

2. **Substitutability**: The boundaries between layers are typically defined by interfaces or well-defined contracts, allowing one layer to be swapped or upgraded independently (e.g., switching from one database vendor to another, or re-skinning the presentation layer for mobile devices).

7.1.2 Common Pitfalls and How Patterns Help

While layering is conceptually straightforward, real-world projects often run into problems:

- **Leakage of Abstractions**: The domain or application layer might inadvertently reference database-specific objects (like SQL entities).
- **Overly Tightly Coupled Layers**: The application layer might directly instantiate concrete classes from the infrastructure layer, ignoring interface boundaries.
- **Rigid Layer Boundaries**: Some teams interpret layered architecture so rigidly that changes require multiple layer modifications, leading to slow iteration.

Well-chosen design patterns mitigate these issues:

1. **Facade**: If a subsystem in the infrastructure layer (e.g., a microservice client, caching system, or an external library) becomes too complex, a **Facade** can hide its intricacies behind a simpler interface. The upper layers see only that facade, preventing them from being entangled in lower-level details.

2. **Abstract Factory** or **Builder**: When the application layer needs to create domain objects that are stored or retrieved differently depending on environment or configuration, a creational pattern ensures that the infrastructure concerns remain behind an abstract interface.

3. **Strategy**: Used to define multiple data persistence strategies that can be selected at runtime. For example, the domain layer might not care whether data is stored in PostgreSQL or a file-based system. A **Strategy** keeps each approach encapsulated, so domain objects call a generic "save" method, not a specific database technology method.

7.1.3 Diagram: Classic Four-Layer Architecture

Below is a textual diagram illustrating how design patterns, particularly from the **Structural** category, can slot into each layer boundary:

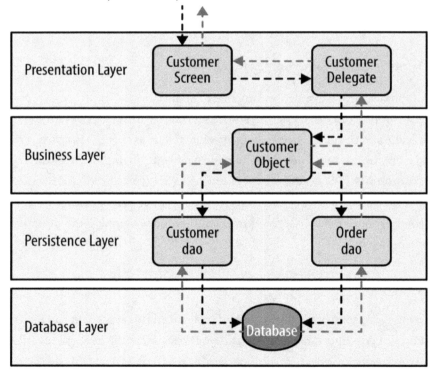

7.1.4 Variations and Trends

Hexagonal Architecture (or Ports and Adapters) refines layering by categorizing layers into "inside" (domain) and "outside" (infrastructure). Adapters talk inward to the domain via ports. Here, patterns like **Adapter** (literally named in the structural patterns) become core building blocks:

each external system has an adapter that conforms to the domain's port interface.

Onion Architecture emphasizes further the domain at the center, with layers swirling outward, ensuring domain code is never aware of technical complexities. Many of the same design patterns— **Factories**, **Repositories**, **Decorators**—reappear to keep external details from leaking in.

7.2 Model-View-Controller (MVC) Pattern

Model-View-Controller (MVC) is an architectural pattern for interactive applications, famously known in GUI frameworks but widely adopted in modern web frameworks. In the classical sense, MVC breaks an application into three interconnected components:

1. **Model**: Manages data, logic, and rules of the application domain.
2. **View**: Renders the model into a UI or output format.
3. **Controller**: Translates user actions or input into operations that manipulate the model or update the view.

7.2.1 Evolving Interpretations of MVC

Although originally introduced for **desktop GUIs**, MVC grew ubiquitous in web frameworks (e.g., Ruby on Rails, ASP.NET MVC, Django). Over time, the pattern diversified:

- **Model** might be pure domain entities or could include data access code, depending on the framework's interpretation.
- **Controller** can be extremely "thin," deferring to "service" or "application" layers, or it may hold extensive logic.
- **View** in server-side frameworks might be HTML templates, while in modern SPAs, the "view" might exist purely on the client side, hooking into JSON or GraphQL data from the server.

7.2.2 Benefits and Architectural Implications

- **Separation of UI and Logic**: The view focuses purely on presentation, while the model retains domain logic.
- **Multiple Views**: A robust MVC design can support multiple presentation layers (e.g., desktop UI, mobile UI) that rely on the same model.
- **Testability**: By isolating domain logic in the model, tests do not require a functioning UI environment.

Yet, poorly executed MVC can lead to **"Massive View Controllers"** (akin to a "God Controller"), or the "Fat Model vs. Skinny Controller" debate, which can overshadow the architectural clarity. This is where design patterns matter: **Strategy** or **Observer** patterns are often embedded in how the model notifies the view, ensuring updates remain consistent.

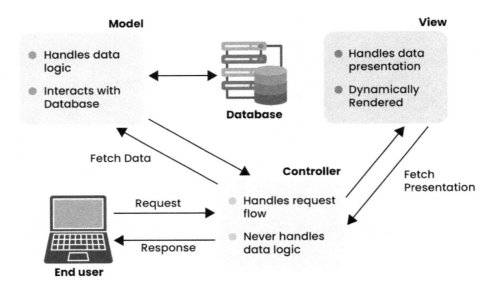

In many MVC frameworks, the "Model" might incorporate or delegate to a separate domain or business layer. The **Controller** orchestrates changes in the Model, and the **View** observes those changes or is explicitly updated by the Controller.

7.2.4 Variants: MVP and MVVM

- **MVP (Model-View-Presenter)**: Primarily used in desktop or mobile contexts. The Presenter mediates between View and Model, with the View delegating virtually all logic to the Presenter.
- **MVVM (Model-View-ViewModel)**: Popular in frameworks like WPF, Angular, or React (conceptually). The ViewModel acts as an observable data context, bridging the "dumb" UI (View) and the Model.

Though named differently, these approaches all embody the same architectural principle of separating concerns. Patterns like **Observer**, **Decorator**, or **Command** often appear under the hood for specific interactions or data binding.

7.3 Dependency Injection and IoC

Dependency Injection (DI) and **Inversion of Control (IoC)** are related concepts that have dramatically shaped modern software architecture. They address a crucial question: **How do**

components acquire the dependencies they need to function? Instead of classes instantiating their own collaborators (hard-coded dependencies), IoC mandates that an external entity (a container or framework) creates and assembles those objects. This approach fosters:

- **Loose Coupling**: Classes rely on abstractions, not concrete implementations.
- **Testability**: Dependencies can be easily swapped with mocks or stubs in testing.
- **Configurable Architectures**: Swapping out entire layers or modules can be done by reconfiguring the DI container rather than rewriting code.

7.3.1 Conceptual Foundations

Prior to IoC, typical code looked like:

```
class Service {
    private Database db;
    public Service() {
        this.db = new MySQLDatabase();
    }
}
```

Here, Service is tightly coupled to MySQLDatabase. With DI, the constructor or setter might accept a Database interface instead, and a separate **IoC container** or a factory method handles which concrete implementation to supply. The Service no longer "knows" about MySQL specifically.

7.3.2 Common DI Techniques

1. **Constructor Injection**: A class receives dependencies via constructor parameters.
2. **Setter Injection**: A class exposes setter methods to inject dependencies after instantiation.
3. **Interface Injection**: An interface method is used to supply dependencies, though less common.

Most enterprise frameworks (e.g., Spring in Java, .NET Core, Angular in TypeScript) provide a **dependency injection container** that automatically resolves and injects dependencies based on configuration or annotations.

7.3.3 Patterns that Align with DI/IoC

- **Factory Method** or **Abstract Factory**: The container effectively acts as a factory, creating objects with correct dependencies.
- **Decorator**: IoC containers can wrap an implementation with a decorator. For instance, a logging decorator might be automatically applied to all service classes.
- **Service Locator**: In older or alternative approaches, the "container" is used imperatively

as a service locator. However, many see service locators as an anti-pattern if used pervasively, since it reintroduces hidden dependencies.

7.3.4 Architectural Implications

Once IoC is in place:

- Each **layer** or **module** can define an interface for how it communicates externally (e.g., domain services, repositories).
- The container configures which concrete classes implement those interfaces, hooking everything together at **composition** time.
- The system becomes more modular, with each piece "pluggable," enabling advanced scenarios like multiple environment configurations, A/B testing strategies, or dynamic reloading of features.

Diagram: Basic IoC Container

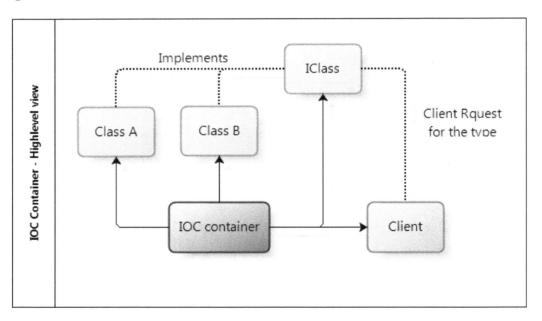

7.4 Event-Driven Architecture and Observer Pattern

In many modern systems—particularly those requiring scalability, responsiveness, or decoupled services—**event-driven** or **message-driven** architectures have become a cornerstone. These architectures revolve around **events** being emitted by one component and **consumed** by others without tight coupling or synchronous blocking. The **Observer** pattern, in spirit, underlies this approach by establishing a publish-subscribe relationship, although event-driven systems typically extend the pattern across processes, machines, or microservices.

7.4.1 The Essence of Event-Driven Architecture

In an event-driven system:

1. **Producers** generate events—these can be domain events like "OrderPlaced" or technical signals like "CacheInvalidation."
2. **Consumers** subscribe to relevant events and react asynchronously, updating local data, initiating workflows, or sending notifications.
3. **Messaging Channels** (topics, queues) or **Event Buses/Brokers** mediate between producers and consumers, avoiding direct references.

Event-Driven Architecture

7.4.2 Mapping Observer to Event-Driven

While the **Observer** pattern (as classically defined) usually applies within a single process—an object subject notifies its observers—modern event-driven systems generalize it:

- **Subject** -> The service or component that triggers domain events.
- **Observer** -> Another service or component that listens and reacts.
- **notifyObservers()** -> In a distributed environment, this is "publish the event to the broker or bus."
- **update()** -> "Consume the event message and act accordingly."

This conceptual alignment means the principles of **low coupling** and **high cohesion** from Observer carry over. The difference is scale: event-driven architecture uses additional middleware (message brokers, streaming platforms) to manage complexity.

7.4.3 Benefits and Architectural Relevance

- **Scalability**: Observers can run on separate nodes or scale horizontally.
- **Fault Tolerance**: If one observer fails, others can continue. The event bus can buffer messages until the failing component is restored.
- **Asynchrony**: Producers do not block waiting on observer processing, which suits high-throughput systems.

However, event-driven design can introduce challenges around **event ordering**, **idempotency**, and **eventual consistency**. Patterns like **Saga** or **Outbox** might be required to handle distributed transactions. Still, the fundamental building blocks echo the **Observer** approach.

7.4.4 Diagram: Simplified Event-Driven Flow

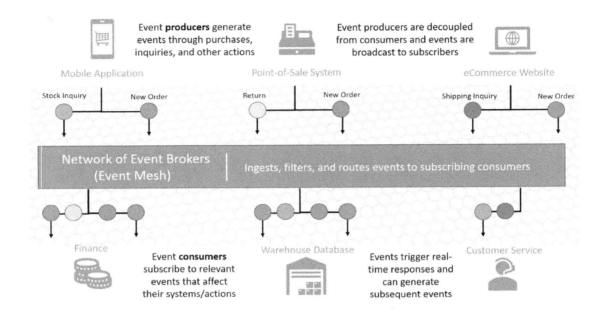

Each microservice or component acts as an observer to events of interest. The bus relays events, decoupling producers from consumers.

7.5 Additional Reflections: Architecture-Pattern Synergy

Design patterns, as originally documented, were based on smaller-scale, object-oriented paradigms. Modern architectures—microservices, serverless, domain-driven design, event sourcing—are typically more **macro-level**. Nonetheless, the synergy remains strong:

1. **Architecture Provides the Skeleton**: The layered or service-oriented structure sets broad boundaries, specifying "what belongs where."

2. **Patterns Fill in the Details**: Within each module or boundary, patterns shape how objects are created (creational), combined (structural), or how they collaborate (behavioral).

3. **Enforcement of Boundaries**: Patterns like **Facade** or **Adapter** ensure that layers or services do not become overly interwoven.

4. **Future-Proofing**: By applying design patterns, an architecture can pivot more gracefully when new technologies or business demands arise.

7.5.1 Aligning with Domain-Driven Design

Domain-Driven Design (DDD) has also gained prominence in bridging architectural concepts with design patterns. For instance:

- **Aggregates** in DDD can be thought of as a cluster of domain objects that are created and managed by a pattern akin to **Factory** or **Builder**.
- **Domain Services** may use **Strategy** to handle variable logic, or **Observer** for domain events.
- **Repositories** in DDD often incorporate **Proxy** or **Adapter** patterns to abstract away the actual database or external system.

While DDD is not a design pattern library per se, it provides context: the architectural emphasis on ubiquitous language and bounded contexts intersects nicely with the structural or behavioral patterns that keep code aligned with the domain model.

7.5.2 Hybrid Approaches

Systems rarely follow a single architectural pattern. A complex enterprise might have:

- A **layered architecture** in each service to keep internal code organized.
- **Event-driven** interactions between services using observer-like messaging.
- **Dependency Injection** containers in each microservice to manage object lifecycles.
- **MVC** or **MVVM** patterns on the front-end for user-facing applications.

This multiplicity can seem daunting but is actually beneficial if each approach is chosen judiciously. Design patterns become the glue that keeps micro-level solutions consistent with each macro-level architectural principle.

7.6 Practical Considerations and Real-World Tips

Although the synergy between design patterns and software architecture sounds straightforward in theory, real-world development teams face complexities that require balancing best practices with practical constraints. Below are some practical considerations:

7.6.1 Don't Over-Engineer

One common pitfall is adopting advanced architectural paradigms or a large arsenal of design patterns for problems that may not need such complexity. The **Golden Hammer** anti-pattern (discussed earlier) warns us not to apply the same pattern everywhere. Similarly, one should not force microservices or layered architecture if a smaller monolithic solution suffices. The key is to weigh **organizational needs**, **scalability demands**, and **domain complexity** before deciding on architecture and pattern usage.

7.6.2 Consistent Pattern Language

When a team adopts design patterns systematically, it gains a shared vocabulary. This is invaluable for describing architecture. Instead of lengthy explanations, a developer can say, "We'll place a Facade around the messaging subsystem to unify internal calls," and others know exactly what that entails. Encourage new team members to learn and reference that pattern vocabulary. Document how the architecture is structured and which patterns apply at each boundary.

7.6.3 Refactoring into Patterns

Not every system starts with a robust architecture. Many codebases evolve organically, leading to an accumulation of ad-hoc solutions. Over time, you can **refactor** code to introduce appropriate design patterns and more coherent layering. For instance, if you discover a "God class" bridging domain logic and database calls, you might break it up into a domain entity (model), a repository (infrastructure), and a service (application layer) with a **Factory Method** for object creation. This refactoring requires careful analysis, but yields a codebase that better aligns with desired architectural norms.

7.6.4 Tooling and Frameworks

Modern frameworks incorporate many design patterns by default:
- **Spring Boot** (Java) or **ASP.NET Core** (.NET) handle **IoC/DI** out of the box, generating typical layered structures.
- **Angular** enforces an **MV**-style approach, with modules, components, and services.
- **Vue.js** or **React** provide structures that can incorporate **MVC** or **MVVM** ideas, often combining them with **Observer** or event-driven patterns for state management.

Leverage the framework's recommended patterns but stay vigilant if your domain or performance constraints differ from the "standard path." It is perfectly acceptable to adapt or override defaults if architecture demands it.

7.6.5 Architecture Reviews and Pattern Audits

Large projects benefit from periodic **architecture reviews**. Teams examine modules, boundaries, and dependencies, checking whether the code still reflects the intended design. Pattern audits can reveal if certain design patterns are missing, misused, or overshadowed by emergent anti-patterns. For instance, a once-layered system might degrade as developers inadvertently add direct calls from the presentation layer to the database. Regular reviews catch these drifts early, so they can be corrected before technical debt multiplies.

Chapter 8: Hands-on Implementation of Design Patterns

Up to now, we have explored what design patterns are, why they matter, and how they fit into architectural choices. But even the most robust theoretical understanding only becomes valuable when you can **implement** these patterns effectively in code. Each programming language has its own idioms, syntactic features, and best practices, which influence how you apply design patterns. This chapter offers a **practical, language-focused** look at how patterns come to life in real projects.

8.1 Implementing Patterns in Java

Java is one of the classic Object-Oriented languages, known for its static typing, extensive standard library, and well-established community frameworks. Java's verbosity encourages developers to be explicit about classes and interfaces, which can make the structure of design patterns quite clear. Moreover, Java frameworks like **Spring** heavily incorporate or facilitate certain patterns (e.g., **Dependency Injection**, **Template Method** in abstract classes), so Java devs often encounter these patterns by default.

8.1.1 Creational Pattern Examples in Java

8.1.1.1 Singleton with Lazy Initialization

While singletons can be overused, it remains illustrative to see how a lazy-loaded singleton is typically done in Java:

```
public class LazySingleton {
```

```
    private static volatile LazySingleton instance;

    private LazySingleton() {
        // private constructor prevents external instantiation
    }

    public static LazySingleton getInstance() {
        if (instance == null) {
            synchronized (LazySingleton.class) {
                if (instance == null) {
                    instance = new LazySingleton();
                }
            }
        }
        return instance;
    }

    public void doSomething() {
        System.out.println("LazySingleton is doing something.");
    }
}
```

Key Points:

- **volatile** ensures that updates to instance are visible across threads.
- **Double-checked locking** is a common idiom in Java to reduce synchronization overhead after initialization.
- For simpler code, some developers prefer **eager loading** or the **static holder** technique.

8.1.1.2 Factory Method

Java's strong class-based structure makes the **Factory Method** pattern straightforward. Suppose we have an interface Notification and multiple implementations:

```
public interface Notification {
    void notifyUser(String message);
}

public class EmailNotification implements Notification {
    @Override
    public void notifyUser(String message) {
```

```
      System.out.println("Sending EMAIL with message: " + message);
   }
}


public class SMSNotification implements Notification {
   @Override
   public void notifyUser(String message) {
      System.out.println("Sending SMS with message: " + message);
   }
}
```

Then the **Creator** (abstract or base class) has a createNotification() method that subclasses override:

```
public abstract class NotificationCreator {
   public void send(String message) {
      Notification notification = createNotification();
      notification.notifyUser(message);
   }

   protected abstract Notification createNotification();
}

public class EmailCreator extends NotificationCreator {
   @Override
   protected Notification createNotification() {
      return new EmailNotification();
   }
}

public class SMSCreator extends NotificationCreator {
   @Override
   protected Notification createNotification() {
      return new SMSNotification();
   }
}
```

Usage:

```
NotificationCreator creator = new EmailCreator();
creator.send("Hello via Email!");


creator = new SMSCreator();
creator.send("Hello via SMS!");
```

Key Points:

- Java's explicit classes and overriding highlight how the factory method is specialized in subclasses.
- Testing each subclass is simpler, as each defines a unique creation logic.

8.1.2 Structural Pattern Examples in Java

8.1.2.1 Decorator

The **Decorator** pattern is well-suited to Java's interface-based approach. For instance, suppose you have:

```
public interface DataSource {
    void writeData(String data);
    String readData();
}
```

A **ConcreteComponent** might be FileDataSource that reads/writes from a file:

```
public class FileDataSource implements DataSource {
    private String filename;

    public FileDataSource(String filename) {
        this.filename = filename;
    }

    @Override
    public void writeData(String data) {
        // ... write data to file
    }

    @Override
    public String readData() {
        // ... read data from file
        return "File contents";
```

```
    }
  }
```

Decorator class:

```
public abstract class DataSourceDecorator implements DataSource {
  protected DataSource wrappee;

  public DataSourceDecorator(DataSource source) {
    this.wrappee = source;
  }

  @Override
  public void writeData(String data) {
    wrappee.writeData(data);
  }

  @Override
  public String readData() {
    return wrappee.readData();
  }
}
```

ConcreteDecorator examples, such as encryption or compression:

```
public class EncryptionDecorator extends DataSourceDecorator {
  public EncryptionDecorator(DataSource source) {
    super(source);
  }

  @Override
  public void writeData(String data) {
    String encrypted = encrypt(data);
    super.writeData(encrypted);
  }

  @Override
  public String readData() {
    String data = super.readData();
```

```
        return decrypt(data);
    }

    private String encrypt(String data) {
        // dummy encryption logic
        return "ENC{" + data + "}";
    }

    private String decrypt(String data) {
        return data.replace("ENC{","").replace("}","");
    }
}
```

Usage:

```
DataSource file = new FileDataSource("data.txt");
DataSource encryptedFile = new EncryptionDecorator(file);

encryptedFile.writeData("Hello Decorator Pattern");
String result = encryptedFile.readData();
System.out.println(result); // Decrypted content
```

Key Points:
- In Java, you frequently see decorators used around InputStream/OutputStream in the standard library, exemplifying how the pattern works in practice.
- Testing is simple: you can directly test the wrapper's input/output with or without decoration.

8.1.3 Behavioral Pattern Examples in Java

8.1.3.1 Observer (with Built-in Java Tools)

While Java has deprecated the older java.util.Observable and Observer classes, you can implement a custom observer pattern or use third-party frameworks (e.g., Reactive Streams). A custom approach:

```
public interface Observer {
    void update(float temperature);
}
```

```java
public class WeatherStation {
    private List<Observer> observers = new ArrayList<>();
    private float temperature;

    public void attach(Observer obs) {
        observers.add(obs);
    }

    public void detach(Observer obs) {
        observers.remove(obs);
    }

    public void setTemperature(float temperature) {
        this.temperature = temperature;
        notifyAllObservers();
    }

    private void notifyAllObservers() {
        for (Observer o : observers) {
            o.update(temperature);
        }
    }
}

public class Display implements Observer {
    @Override
    public void update(float temperature) {
        System.out.println("Display updated: " + temperature);
    }
}
```

Key Points:
- Decouples the WeatherStation from the details of how the Display (or any observer) handles the update.
- In Java, frameworks like Spring can leverage event listeners to approximate a more advanced observer pattern across components.

8.2 Implementing Patterns in Python

Python is dynamically typed, supporting both procedural and object-oriented styles, as well as first-class functions and decorators at the language level. Some design patterns translate quite differently compared to Java, thanks to Python's flexibility and succinct syntax. However, the patterns' essence remains the same.

8.2.1 Creational Pattern Examples in Python

8.2.1.1 Singleton (Using a Metaclass or a Module)

Because Python modules themselves are singleton-like (loaded once per interpreter session), a trivial way to achieve a "singleton" effect is to store data at the module scope. Alternatively, you can use a **metaclass**:

```python
class SingletonMeta(type):
    _instances = {}
    def __call__(cls, *args, **kwargs):
        if cls not in cls._instances:
            cls._instances[cls] = super(SingletonMeta, cls).__call__(*args, **kwargs)
        return cls._instances[cls]

class Logger(metaclass=SingletonMeta):
    def __init__(self):
        self.logs = []

    def log(self, message):
        self.logs.append(message)

# Usage
logger1 = Logger()
logger2 = Logger()
print(logger1 is logger2)  # True
```

Key Points:

- Metaclasses let you intercept class instantiation to enforce a single instance.
- This approach can be surprising if devs are not familiar with Python's metaprogramming features.

8.2.1.2 Factory Function (Simple Approach)

Python often uses functions instead of classes for factories:

```python
class EmailNotification:
```

```python
    def notify_user(self, message):
        print(f"Email: {message}")

class SMSNotification:
    def notify_user(self, message):
        print(f"SMS: {message}")

def notification_factory(method="email"):
    if method == "email":
        return EmailNotification()
    elif method == "sms":
        return SMSNotification()
    else:
        raise ValueError("Unknown notification method")
```

Usage:

```python
notif = notification_factory("email")
notif.notify_user("Hello via Python factory!")
```

Key Points:

- Dynamic typing means you don't always need an interface.
- Enums or config data can be used to manage multiple "product" types.

8.2.2 Structural Pattern Examples in Python

8.2.2.1 Decorator (Using Python's Built-in Decorator Syntax)

Python's language-level decorators are different from the "decorator design pattern," but they share conceptual similarities. Here we focus on the traditional OO decorator, wrapping an object:

```python
import json

class DataSource:
    def write_data(self, data: str):
        pass

    def read_data(self) -> str:
        pass

class FileDataSource(DataSource):
```

```python
    def __init__(self, filename):
        self._filename = filename

    def write_data(self, data: str):
        with open(self._filename, 'w') as file:
            file.write(data)

    def read_data(self) -> str:
        with open(self._filename, 'r') as file:
            return file.read()

class DataSourceDecorator(DataSource):
    def __init__(self, source: DataSource):
        self._wrappee = source

    def write_data(self, data: str):
        self._wrappee.write_data(data)

    def read_data(self) -> str:
        return self._wrappee.read_data()

class EncryptionDecorator(DataSourceDecorator):
    def write_data(self, data: str):
        encrypted = self._encrypt(data)
        super().write_data(encrypted)

    def read_data(self) -> str:
        data = super().read_data()
        return self._decrypt(data)

    def _encrypt(self, data):
        return json.dumps({"encrypted": data})

    def _decrypt(self, data):
        obj = json.loads(data)
        return obj["encrypted"]
```

Usage:

```
file_ds = FileDataSource("test.txt")
encrypted_ds = EncryptionDecorator(file_ds)

encrypted_ds.write_data("Sensitive info")
print(encrypted_ds.read_data())  # "Sensitive info"
```

Key Points:

- In Python, it is easy to test various decorators by instantiating them at runtime.
- If you prefer a functional approach, you might use a **callable** object or function decorators, but that's more akin to code-level decorators than the structural design pattern.

8.2.3 Behavioral Pattern Examples in Python

8.2.3.1 Strategy (Using First-Class Functions)

Python's functions are first-class objects. We can exploit this to implement a strategy-like approach:

```python
def quick_sort(data):
    # placeholder quicksort logic
    return sorted(data)  # ironically uses built-in sort

def merge_sort(data):
    # placeholder mergesort logic
    return sorted(data)

class Sorter:
    def __init__(self, strategy=quick_sort):
        self.strategy = strategy

    def set_strategy(self, strategy_func):
        self.strategy = strategy_func

    def sort_data(self, data):
        return self.strategy(data)

# Usage
sorter = Sorter()
result = sorter.sort_data([4,1,7,3])
print("QuickSort:", result)
```

```
sorter.set_strategy(merge_sort)
print("MergeSort:", sorter.sort_data([4,1,7,3]))
```

Key Points:
- This approach is extremely concise, leveraging Python's dynamic nature.
- Alternatively, you can implement each strategy in a class that implements a sort method, mimicking classical OOP designs.

8.3 Implementing Patterns in C++

C++ is a low-level, statically typed language that allows for both object-oriented and generic programming. While design patterns remain relevant, C++ intricacies—like memory management, templates, and multiple inheritance—can complicate or sometimes simplify pattern implementations.

8.3.1 Creational Pattern Examples in C++

8.3.1.1 Abstract Factory with Product Families

C++ can use pure virtual functions to define product interfaces. Suppose we have two families of "GUI" elements: Windows style and Mac style.

```cpp
// Abstract Product Interfaces
class Button {
public:
    virtual void render() = 0;
    virtual ~Button() {}
};

class TextField {
public:
    virtual void display() = 0;
    virtual ~TextField() {}
};

// Concrete Products: Windows
class WinButton : public Button {
public:
    void render() override {
```

```cpp
      std::cout << "Render Windows Button\n";
  }
};

class WinTextField : public TextField {
public:
  void display() override {
    std::cout << "Display Windows Text Field\n";
  }
};

// Concrete Products: Mac
class MacButton : public Button {
public:
  void render() override {
    std::cout << "Render Mac Button\n";
  }
};

class MacTextField : public TextField {
public:
  void display() override {
    std::cout << "Display Mac Text Field\n";
  }
};

// Abstract Factory
class GUIFactory {
public:
  virtual Button* createButton() = 0;
  virtual TextField* createTextField() = 0;
  virtual ~GUIFactory() {}
};

// Concrete Factories
class WinFactory : public GUIFactory {
public:
  Button* createButton() override {
    return new WinButton();
```

```cpp
    }
    TextField* createTextField() override {
        return new WinTextField();
    }
};

class MacFactory : public GUIFactory {
public:
    Button* createButton() override {
        return new MacButton();
    }
    TextField* createTextField() override {
        return new MacTextField();
    }
};

// Usage Example
int main() {
    GUIFactory* factory = new WinFactory();
    Button* btn = factory->createButton();
    btn->render();

    TextField* tf = factory->createTextField();
    tf->display();

    delete btn;
    delete tf;
    delete factory;

    return 0;
}
```

Key Points:

- Manual memory management is used here. Real production code might use **smart pointers**.
- Each factory method calls new for specific product classes.
- This pattern is powerful when you have multiple families of related products (e.g., different OS themes).

8.3.2.1 Adapter with Multiple Inheritance

C++ supports multiple inheritance, which can implement a **class adapter** variant. Suppose we have:

```cpp
class LegacyRectangle {
public:
    void drawLegacy(int x1, int y1, int x2, int y2) {
        std::cout << "Drawing rectangle from (" << x1 << "," << y1 <<
                ") to (" << x2 << "," << y2 << ")\n";
    }
};

class RectInterface {
public:
    virtual void draw(int x, int y, int width, int height) = 0;
    virtual ~RectInterface() {}
};

// Class adapter: inherits from both the interface and the adaptee
class RectangleAdapter : public RectInterface, private LegacyRectangle {
public:
    void draw(int x, int y, int width, int height) override {
        drawLegacy(x, y, x + width, y + height);
    }
};

int main() {
    RectInterface* rect = new RectangleAdapter();
    rect->draw(10, 20, 40, 30);
    delete rect;
    return 0;
}
```

Key Points:
- The adapter inherits from RectInterface publicly and from LegacyRectangle privately.
- We have direct access to drawLegacy() from the base class.
- Must carefully manage object lifetimes as usual in C++.

8.3.3.1 Command with Undo

C++ command objects might store states for undo operations. For instance:

```cpp
class Command {
public:
  virtual void execute() = 0;
  virtual void undo() = 0;
  virtual ~Command() {}
};

class Document {
  std::string content;
public:
  void setContent(const std::string& c) { content = c; }
  std::string getContent() const { return content; }
};

class AppendCommand : public Command {
  Document* doc;
  std::string text;
  size_t previousSize;
public:
  AppendCommand(Document* d, const std::string& t) : doc(d), text(t), previousSize(0) {}

  void execute() override {
    previousSize = doc->getContent().size();
    doc->setContent(doc->getContent() + text);
  }

  void undo() override {
    auto current = doc->getContent();
    doc->setContent(current.substr(0, previousSize));
  }
};

// Usage
int main() {
```

```cpp
    Document doc;
    AppendCommand cmd(&doc, "Hello C++ Command!");
    cmd.execute();
    std::cout << doc.getContent() << std::endl;
    cmd.undo();
    std::cout << doc.getContent() << std::endl;
    return 0;
}
```

Key Points:

- The Command must store any necessary state to revert changes.
- The client or an "invoker" can keep a history of commands for multi-step undo.
- C++ code often requires care around object ownership (e.g., a raw pointer Document* vs. a std::shared_ptr<Document>).

8.4 Implementing Patterns in JavaScript

JavaScript is a dynamically typed, prototype-based language widely used for web front-end development, Node.js back ends, and beyond. Patterns must be adapted to JavaScript's functional and prototype-based nature. ES6+ syntax can mimic classical OOP, but the language also offers other styles.

8.4.1 Creational Pattern Examples in JavaScript

8.4.1.1 Module Pattern for Singleton

In JavaScript, modules are singletons by default because each imported module is cached as a single instance. Alternatively, you can define an object literal that behaves like a singleton:

```javascript
// logger.js
const Logger = (function() {
 let logs = [];
 function log(message) {
  logs.push(message);
  console.log("Log:", message);
 }
 function getCount() {
  return logs.length;
 }
 return {
  log,
```

```
    getCount
  };
})();


module.exports = Logger;

// usage in another file
const logger1 = require('./logger');
const logger2 = require('./logger');
logger1.log("First log");
console.log(logger2.getCount()); // 1, same instance
```

Key Points:

- This pattern is straightforward in Node.js due to the way module caching works.
- For front-end, you might store singletons in a single script import or as a globally accessible object in some frameworks.

8.4.1.2 Factory with Object Literals

```
function createNotification(type) {
  switch(type) {
    case 'email':
      return {
        notifyUser: (msg) => console.log(`Email: ${msg}`)
      };
    case 'sms':
      return {
        notifyUser: (msg) => console.log(`SMS: ${msg}`)
      };
    default:
      throw new Error('Unknown notification type');
  }
}

// usage
const emailNotif = createNotification('email');
emailNotif.notifyUser("Hello from JS factory!");
```

Key Points:

- JavaScript's ability to return object literals on the fly makes factories quite concise.
- If needed, you could define classes and new them instead of returning object literals.

8.4.2 Structural Pattern Examples in JavaScript

8.4.2.1 Decorator with Function Wrapping

While OO decorators can be done using classes and prototypes, a more idiomatic JavaScript approach is function wrapping, especially in Node.js or an ES environment:

```javascript
function readFile(filePath) {
  // a simple function to read file content (mock)
  return "File content from " + filePath;
}

function readFileWithCache(fn) {
  const cache = {};
  return function(filePath) {
    if (cache[filePath]) {
      console.log("Returning cached result for", filePath);
      return cache[filePath];
    }
    const result = fn(filePath);
    cache[filePath] = result;
    return result;
  };
}

// usage
const cachedRead = readFileWithCache(readFile);
console.log(cachedRead("test.txt"));
console.log(cachedRead("test.txt")); // returns from cache
```

Here, we decorate the readFile function with caching logic. This is akin to the structural design pattern: we have the same interface (a function that takes filePath and returns content) but with augmented behavior.

8.4.3 Behavioral Pattern Examples in JavaScript

8.4.3.1 Observer (Event Emitter)

JavaScript on the client side frequently uses events (DOM events) to achieve an observer-like mechanism. On Node.js, the built-in **EventEmitter** class can be leveraged:

163

```javascript
const EventEmitter = require('events');

class WeatherStation extends EventEmitter {
  constructor() {
    super();
    this.temperature = 0;
  }

  setTemperature(temp) {
    this.temperature = temp;
    this.emit('temperatureChanged', temp);
  }
}

class Display {
  update(temp) {
    console.log("Display updated to: " + temp);
  }
}

// usage
const station = new WeatherStation();
const display = new Display();

// subscribe
station.on('temperatureChanged', (temp) => display.update(temp));

station.setTemperature(25);
station.setTemperature(30);
```

Key Points:

- This approach is effectively the **Observer** pattern, with EventEmitter acting as the subject.
- Very common in Node.js, and front-end code often uses variations like the DOM's addEventListener.

8.5 Testing and Integration Considerations

Regardless of language, design pattern implementations should be supported by robust **testing**.

Here are a few universal tips:

1. **Isolate Each Participant**: For example, if you are testing a **Decorator**, ensure you have a mock or simplified "wrappee" to confirm the decorator's behavior.

2. **Mocking Dependencies**: In patterns like **Factory** or **Prototype**, you can mock the creation steps to ensure your code calls them as expected.

3. **End-to-End**: Some patterns, like **Observer** or **Command**, can be tested end-to-end by simulating events or command invocations, verifying that the system transitions states as intended.

Integration is simpler if your design patterns remain well-defined and do not sprawl across unrelated modules. For instance, if you have a microservice architecture (as discussed in prior chapters), each microservice might internally use **Factory** or **Singleton**. Keep those patterns locally consistent and documented, so other services or teams can integrate without confusion.

8.6 Common Pitfalls in Implementing Patterns

8.6.1 Overcomplicating Code with Patterns

A pattern is a tool, not a mandatory rule. If you find that your code becomes more convoluted after applying a pattern, reconsider whether a simpler approach (e.g., a single function or a direct method call) is enough.

8.6.2 Neglecting Language Idioms

For instance, writing a verbose Java-like singleton in Python might look awkward and ignore simpler module-level approaches. Similarly, forcing a purely functional approach in C++ might hamper clarity if your team expects OOP solutions. Each language has idiomatic ways to implement patterns.

8.6.3 Inconsistent Naming or Structure

Patterns rely on well-known class or method naming to be recognized easily by collaborators. If you call your builder method "makeThingy" in one place and "createObject" in another, you risk confusion. Keep naming consistent and reflect the pattern's standard terms.

8.6.4 Testing Blind Spots

Some design patterns revolve around dynamic behavior (e.g., **State**, **Strategy**, or **Observer**). You must test transitions thoroughly. For example, if your **State** pattern changes from "Idle" to "Active," confirm that the methods behave differently in each state.

8.7 Sample Diagrams of Cross-Language Pattern Comparisons

To visualize how the same pattern might look in different languages, consider a **Factory** pattern used for shape creation:

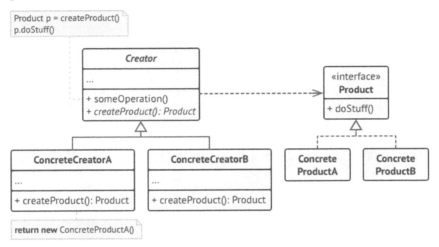

The **factory pattern** defers instantiation logic of a parent abstract class to its concrete sub-classes. At the time of object creation, the specific class type may not be known, in which a creator class' factory method is used to decouple this identifying logic. This is typically done through the methods, parameters, and a switch statement.

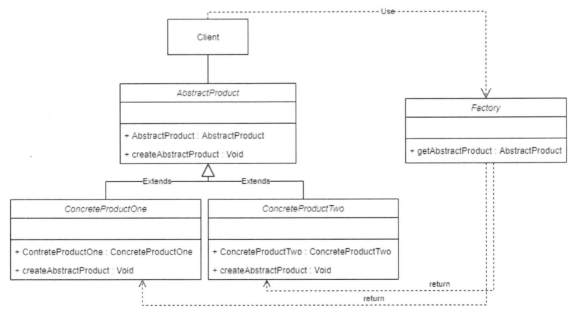

FactoryPatternDemo, our demo class will use ShapeFactory to get a Shape object. It will pass information (CIRCLE / RECTANGLE / SQUARE) to ShapeFactory to get the type of object it needs.

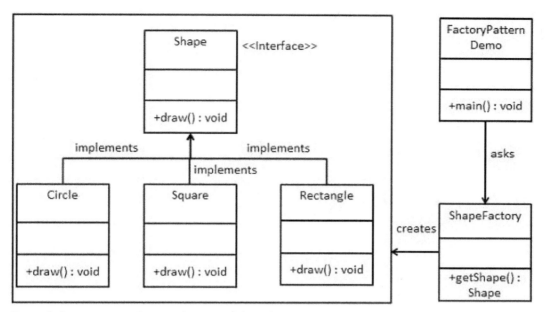

In each language, we have a function/class that returns a shape object. The differences lie in syntax, type usage, and the style of returning or referencing objects.

Chapter 9: Case Studies of Design Patterns in Real-World Projects

By the time design patterns are introduced in many textbooks, the examples often remain somewhat abstract—small code snippets or simplified analogies—without demonstrating the scale and complexity of commercial software or widely adopted open-source systems. In practice, design patterns might not appear in a textbook-perfect form. Instead, developers may adapt or extend patterns to suit domain constraints, technology stacks, performance targets, or organizational processes.

9.1 Enterprise Applications

Enterprise applications are those that typically serve **corporate, government, or organizational** needs, often dealing with sensitive data, complex processes, or large user bases. These applications can be anything from **ERP (Enterprise Resource Planning)** to **CRM (Customer Relationship Management)** or specialized domain systems like healthcare management software. Because these systems often persist for years (or decades), the use of strong design patterns is central to **long-term maintainability**, **robustness**, and **scalability**.

9.1.1 Layered Architectures and Patterns in Enterprise Apps

Many enterprise applications adopt a **layered** or **hexagonal** architecture to separate concerns—presentation, application/service, domain, and infrastructure. Within these layers, **design patterns** frequently appear:

1. **Service Layer + Factory**: Enterprise apps often define a service layer that orchestrates domain operations. When creating complex domain objects—like orders, invoices, or user

profiles—**Factory** or **Builder** patterns ensure consistent initialization with the correct business rules.

2. **Repository** (in Domain-Driven Design) or **DAO** (Data Access Object): While "Repository" and "DAO" are domain-driven or enterprise patterns, they often incorporate or are combined with standard design patterns such as **Proxy** or **Abstract Factory** to handle the multiple data sources.

3. **Adapter** for Integrations: Enterprise software frequently integrates with third-party services, legacy systems, or external partners. An **Adapter** can unify these diverse APIs behind an internal interface, preventing changes in external systems from rippling through the entire codebase.

Diagram: Typical Enterprise Layers with Patterns

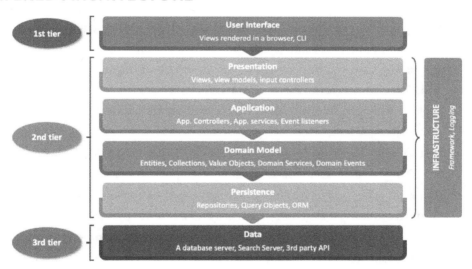

Case Example: In a CRM system that manages thousands of customer records, the domain layer might define a Customer entity. A **Factory** ensures each new Customer is assigned a unique ID, validated for contact info, etc. The application layer calls a Repository (which might be an **Adapter** to an underlying SQL or NoSQL database) to fetch or store these entities. Meanwhile, the presentation layer deals with REST endpoints or a web UI. If the system must integrate with an external marketing service, it uses an **Adapter** to translate the marketing API's data format into internal domain objects.

9.1.2 Use of Behavioral Patterns to Streamline Workflows

Enterprise applications often revolve around processes or **workflows** that can be quite intricate—e.g., an invoice approval might pass through finance, management, and external audits.

Behavioral patterns like **Chain of Responsibility**, **Observer**, or **Command** come into play:

- **Chain of Responsibility**: Each department in an approval process might form a link in the chain, deciding whether to approve, reject, or escalate a request. The client code (or the service layer) only initiates the chain.
- **Observer**: Once a transaction or data update occurs, multiple watchers—e.g., audit logs, analytics modules—are notified automatically, ensuring no duplication of logic.
- **Command**: For enterprise tasks requiring logging, undo/redo, or an action queue, a command approach ensures each operation (like "register new user," "update order status") is encapsulated and can be replayed, audited, or rolled back.

9.1.3 Example: A Large Banking System

Scenario: A multinational bank deploys an internal platform to process loans, track transactions, and handle compliance.

- **Builder Pattern**: Complex domain objects like "LoanApplication" might require step-by-step construction, referencing applicant details, credit scores, collateral data, etc. The builder ensures partial data can be validated before finalizing the object.
- **Observer**: The bank's anti-fraud department is one observer, the credit risk department is another. Each department sees a notification when a new transaction over a certain threshold is processed, allowing them to react without the main system being aware of each department's logic.
- **Bridge**: Certain functionalities (e.g., generating PDF statements vs. HTML statements) might be bridged, decoupling the content generation from the output format.
- **Singleton**: Logging or configuration managers might be singletons—although developers must remain cautious to avoid over-reliance (as discussed in previous anti-pattern sections).

Real Impact: By employing these patterns systematically, the bank can maintain a clean separation of financial logic from compliance checks, code remains testable, and new requirements—like additional notification channels or new loan application steps—can be integrated with minimal disruption to existing code.

9.2 Open-Source Software

Open-source software projects often gather contributions from diverse developers worldwide. In such decentralized environments, clear design patterns help **sustain consistency** and **communicability** across the codebase. Contributors can quickly grasp a project's structure and see how new features should integrate, thanks to recognized patterns.

9.2.1 Pattern-Conscious Projects

Some well-known open-source projects explicitly mention design patterns in their documentation, guiding contributors on:

- **Where to place new classes**
- **Which interfaces or abstract classes** to implement
- **How to handle extension or integration points** (e.g., using **Template Method** or **Strategy** for plugin systems)

This fosters a shared "pattern language" that volunteers can learn and follow, reducing friction in code reviews.

9.2.2 Example: A Popular Web Framework

Django (Python), **Ruby on Rails**, and **Laravel** (PHP) each incorporate patterns:

- **MVC (or MVC-like)**: They enforce a separation where models define data structures, views handle presentation logic, and controllers or actions handle requests.
- **Factory** or **Builder**: Where objects need to be dynamically created, frameworks typically provide factories or "fixture" systems (especially for testing).
- **Template Method**: This pattern often appears in how frameworks let developers override steps in a request lifecycle (e.g., hooking pre-validation logic or customizing rendering).

Django specifically:

1. **Models**: Classes that define database tables.
2. **Views**: Functions or classes receiving HTTP requests.
3. **Template**: The HTML rendering.
4. **Signals** (akin to **Observer** pattern): Let parts of the system be notified when certain model actions occur (e.g., "post_save" signals).

Because these patterns are baked in, new contributors quickly adapt. They do not have to invent new approaches for hooking into model changes or overriding request flows.

9.2.3 Example: A Collaborative Editor

Consider an open-source code editor, such as **VS Code**'s extension ecosystem, or older projects like **Eclipse**. They rely heavily on:

- **Plugin Mechanisms: Observer** or **Mediator** patterns handle plugin events, allowing them to respond to file changes or UI interactions.
- **Command**: Each editor action or extension might register commands that appear in menus or the command palette, encapsulating logic to be undone or repeated.
- **Composite**: The UI layout might treat views and panels as composite objects, enabling complex docking or hierarchical arrangement.

Diagram: Editor with Plugin System

This structure ensures that new plugins do not need to modify the core editor code. They simply **observe** relevant events or register **commands** to be invoked by the user.

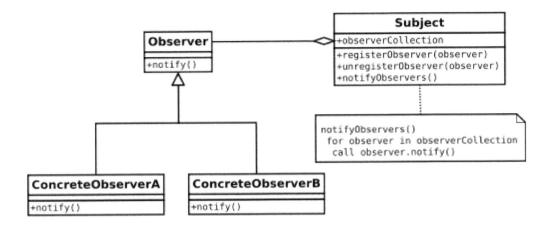

Each plugin registers to events from the core editor, implementing the Observer pattern.

9.2.4 Impact on Community and Maintenance

Open-source maintainers emphasize patterns because they:

- **Facilitate Code Reviews**: Maintainers can quickly spot if a contributor's patch adheres to the established pattern or not.
- **Simplify Onboarding**: The project readme or wiki can say, "We use the Strategy pattern for new rendering approaches," so new devs replicate the same structure.
- **Ensure Extendibility**: By building core modules with patterns like **Facade** or **Adapter**, the software can adapt to new platforms or data formats without rewriting major subsystems.

9.3 Large-Scale Systems

Large-scale systems push design patterns to their limits. "Large-scale" might refer to:

- **High concurrency**: Tens of thousands or millions of concurrent users or requests.
- **Vast domain complexity**: Intricate business logic spanning many subdomains.
- **Geographically distributed**: Data centers around the world, microservices architecture.

In such contexts, patterns that handle **distribution, resilience**, and **event-driven** architectures become crucial. While classic patterns like **Observer** or **Factory** remain relevant, they often appear as **distributed** or **cloud** variants.

9.3.1 Microservices and Patterns

When an application is decomposed into dozens or hundreds of microservices, you see patterns like:

- **Proxy** or **Gateway**: A single "API Gateway" or BFF (Backend for Frontend) serves as a

Facade that routes requests to microservices. This is a structural pattern at the system level.

- **Circuit Breaker**: This is not among the original "Gang of Four," but it acts similarly to a **Proxy** that monitors service calls, "opening" to short-circuit them if repeated failures occur.
- **Saga**: A specialized pattern for distributed transactions or workflows, loosely reminiscent of **Chain of Responsibility** across services, each step committing or compensating.

9.3.2 Case Example: E-Commerce at Scale

A major e-commerce platform (e.g., **Amazon, Alibaba,** or smaller parallels) typically uses:

1. **Service Architecture**: Each domain area (catalog, inventory, payments, shipping, recommendations) is a separate microservice.
2. **Event-Driven** Interactions: Observers or **publish-subscribe** ensures that when an order is placed, multiple microservices react—updating inventory, sending shipping notifications, adjusting recommendation data.
3. **Strategy** for Recommender Engines: The site can switch among multiple recommendation algorithms depending on the product category or user history. Each algorithm is a "strategy," providing a standardized interface for retrieving results.
4. **Flyweight** for Caching Product Data: Millions of product objects exist, but many share images, descriptions, or pricing logic. A flyweight approach might store shared data once, with extrinsic state referencing it.

In practice, these patterns ensure the e-commerce site remains responsive at scale, can adapt to new demands (like flash sales or new shipping providers), and isolates failures to avoid global outages.

Diagram: Simplified E-Commerce Microservices

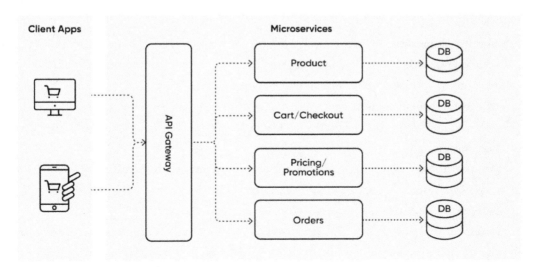

This gateway might function similarly to a **Facade** or **Proxy**, coordinating calls. Each service can also broadcast domain events (like "OrderPlaced"), which others observe or subscribe to.

9.3.3 Domain Complexity and Patterns in Large-Scale Systems

Domain-driven approaches come to the fore in large-scale systems with multiple bounded contexts. Within each context:

- **Aggregate** roots might use **Factory** or **Builder** for consistent creation.
- **Observer**-like event raising in domain models.
- **State** pattern for objects that transition across multiple statuses (like "Pending," "Approved," "Shipped," "Returned" in a logistics domain).

Decorator or **Facade** might handle cross-cutting concerns like caching or logging. Each part of the domain can be swapped or extended if the patterns are well-chosen, ensuring the system can evolve over time without incurring crippling technical debt.

9.3.4 Performance and Scaling

While design patterns help organization and clarity, large-scale systems also worry about **performance**. Overusing certain patterns (like an excessive chain of decorators) can degrade throughput if each invocation triggers multiple object layers. Similarly, naive use of **Singleton** might cause concurrency bottlenecks. Skilled architects measure and tune the pattern usage to ensure they do not hamper the system's performance requirements.

9.4 Observations on the Benefits of Patterns in Practice

Across enterprise, open-source, and large-scale domains, certain **recurring benefits** of design patterns manifest:

1. **Shared Vocabulary**: Teams, even large or decentralized ones, can communicate about solutions quickly by referencing patterns. "We'll adopt a chain-of-responsibility approach for request approval," or "We can inject a logging decorator."
2. **Maintainability**: Systems with clear pattern usage are simpler to refactor, test, and onboard new developers. Patterns anchor code into well-known structures rather than ad-hoc designs.
3. **Adaptability**: Patterns like **Abstract Factory**, **Strategy**, or **Facade** excel at absorbing changes—whether it's a new data store, new algorithm, or evolving external API. The pattern partitions change, so it doesn't cascade unpredictably.
4. **Integration**: Patterns that unify or abstract external services (e.g., **Adapter**, **Proxy**) reduce the friction of hooking new components into a system or bridging legacy code.

Despite these advantages, real-world usage of design patterns can pose challenges:

- **Over-Engineering**: If developers see patterns as mandatory, they may add excessive complexity. The "Golden Hammer" anti-pattern can appear if a favored pattern is forced into every scenario.

- **Mismatch with Domain**: Patterns must align with domain logic. For example, forcing a "Singleton" for an object that truly needs multiple instances can cause confusion or concurrency issues.

- **Evolving Requirements**: Sometimes, a pattern chosen at system inception may no longer be ideal. Continual refactoring and architecture reviews are necessary to keep the system healthy.

9.5 Lessons Learned from Real-World Projects

After examining these case studies and broader usage scenarios, the **key lessons** for adopting design patterns in real-world projects include:

1. **Start with Simplicity**: Patterns are best introduced **incrementally**. Overburdening an early-stage system with advanced patterns can hamper progress.

2. **Document the Pattern's Purpose**: When you adopt a pattern, ensure team members or contributors know *why*. Provide architecture diagrams, code examples, or short design docs clarifying the pattern's role.

3. **Combine Patterns Wisely**: Real systems rarely use just one pattern. For instance, an e-commerce microservice might use **Strategy** for payment methods, **Observer** for inventory updates, and **Facade** for external shipping. The synergy is more important than each pattern's purity.

4. **Refactor Toward Patterns**: Many established projects did not start with a crisp pattern-based design. They refactored into patterns when code smells or domain changes made it clear that a more robust structure was needed.

5. **Leverage Framework Support**: Modern frameworks (like Spring, Angular, Django, .NET Core) embed certain patterns—**Dependency Injection**, **Event** systems, **MVC** layers. Use these built-in patterns to reduce boilerplate and keep your code consistent with the broader ecosystem.

6. **Monitor Performance**: In large-scale systems, patterns that add layers or abstractions can degrade performance. Profile, measure, and optimize if layering becomes too deep or if concurrency in a certain pattern leads to bottlenecks.

Chapter 10: Future of Design Patterns

Design patterns have flourished for several decades, evolving from initial object-oriented contexts to underpinning everything from enterprise-scale systems to microservice architectures and front-end frameworks. As technology and methodologies continue to transform, so too must the patterns that guide us to write maintainable, flexible, and robust code. Moreover, new paradigms—from **functional programming** to **cloud-native microservices**—challenge classical "Gang of Four" patterns, encouraging them to mutate, combine, or be replaced by more specialized approaches.

10.1 Design Patterns and Artificial Intelligence

The past decade has seen **machine learning** (ML), **deep learning**, and **large language models** (LLMs) become major disruptors. Traditional design patterns emerged in a world of deterministic logic, well-defined flows, and explicit algorithmic steps. Today, many software systems incorporate components that rely on data-driven model inferences rather than purely coded logic. How might design patterns evolve or expand to support AI-driven modules?

10.1.1 Patterns for Model Lifecycle Management

A typical ML pipeline includes data collection, preprocessing, model training, validation, deployment, and continuous updates. Each step can become a sub-component of a larger software system. We might see patterns akin to:

- **Model Factory**: Extending the **Factory** concept so that different ML models (e.g., linear regression, random forest, neural network) can be instantiated and configured for training or inference. This "Model Factory" might handle cross-cutting concerns like hardware acceleration or hyperparameter defaults.
- **Observer** for Data Drift**: In production, a model may degrade if the input data

distribution changes. An **Observer**-like mechanism can monitor model performance metrics in real-time. If drift is detected, it notifies a pipeline or triggers a retraining process.

Diagram: High-Level AI Pipeline with Pattern-Like Elements

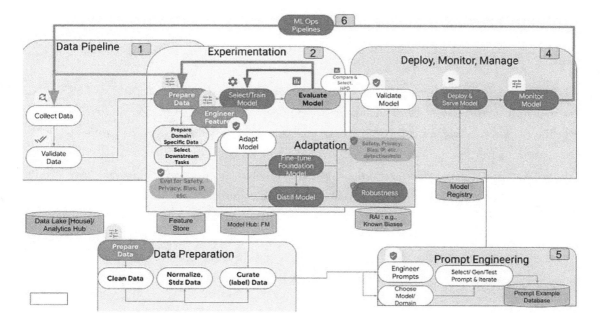

10.1.2 Adaptive Systems and Policy Patterns

AI-based systems often require **adaptive** or **policy-based** logic that changes behavior according to learned insights. For instance, a web service might adopt a "**Strategy**" pattern at runtime, picking the best recommendation algorithm based on current user data. Or a reinforcement learning agent might effectively "edit" the code path at run-time through learned policies.

In the future, we might see patterns specifically addressing:

- **Policy Updaters**: Components that hot-swap or update the logic used by controllers, reminiscent of the **State** pattern, but driven by ML signals.

- **Explainability Decorators**: Wrap black-box models with a "decorator" that captures or logs interpretability data, bridging the gap between inferences and user understanding.

10.1.3 AI-Assisted Pattern Generation

Another angle is how AI tools (like code generation or refactoring assistants) might automatically suggest or implement design patterns. Large language models can parse an entire codebase, detect code smells, and propose a "Refactor to Strategy" or "Extract Decorator." This synergy could drastically reduce the time it takes to adopt patterns or maintain them across big projects. We can imagine advanced IDE integrations that, upon detecting repetitive or overly complex code, prompt a "Would you like to apply the Decorator pattern here?"

10.2 Patterns in Cloud Computing and Serverless

Cloud-native development has redefined how we package, deploy, and scale applications. Patterns that once lived purely at the code level now expand to the domain of infrastructure, orchestration, and ephemeral resources. This fosters new design concerns:

10.2.1 Microservices: Patterns at Scale

We've already seen how microservices architecture often uses structural patterns like **Facade** (in the form of API gateways) or **Adapter** (wrapping external services behind unified interfaces). But the rise of **serverless** platforms—where you only write functions triggered by events—takes these patterns further:

1. **Event-Driven**: Many serverless systems revolve around event triggers (akin to the **Observer** pattern) at the infrastructure level: a file upload to a cloud storage bucket triggers a function, or a message in a queue triggers a data processing job.

2. **Function Chaining** (akin to **Chain of Responsibility**): In serverless workflows, multiple functions might pass data along, each deciding if the next stage should be invoked. This is reminiscent of the **Chain of Responsibility** but implemented as ephemeral cloud functions that spin up on demand.

10.2.2 Infrastructure as Code (IaC) and Patterns

With tools like **Terraform**, **AWS CloudFormation**, or **Pulumi**, entire infrastructures are described in code. We see pattern-like structures in these IaC scripts:

- **Modules** as a form of **Facade**: Hide the complexity of multiple underlying resources (e.g., load balancers, autoscaling groups, security groups) behind a single module interface.

- **Decorator**-like layering: IaC can wrap existing configurations with additional monitoring, logging, or security aspects, similarly to how decorators add responsibilities in code.

10.2.3 Multi-Cloud and Hybrid Patterns

Enterprises might deploy services across multiple cloud providers or maintain on-premises data centers. Patterns can unify these differences:

- **Abstract Factory** for Cloud Deployments: A single interface that can produce "ComputeResource," "DatabaseResource," or "MessageQueue" objects for different providers, enabling the same code to run on AWS, Azure, or GCP with minimal changes.

- **Proxy** for Cross-Cloud Access: A multi-cloud load balancer acts as a proxy, distributing requests to different regions or providers based on cost, latency, or reliability metrics.

In the future, as "cloud sprawl" intensifies, such patterns will become even more critical to unify ephemeral resources in a consistent, maintainable manner.

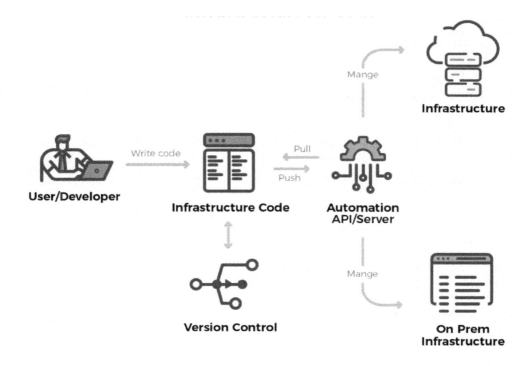

10.3 Functional Programming and Patterns

Most classic design patterns were described with object-oriented languages in mind, focusing on classes, inheritance, and object responsibilities. Over the last decade, **functional programming** (FP) has gained significant traction, driven by languages like **Haskell**, **Scala**, **Elixir**, **F#**, or functional-friendly frameworks in JavaScript. Many patterns either transform or become unnecessary in a purely functional style. However, new or hybrid patterns also emerge.

10.3.1 Patterns that Evolve or Disappear

- **Singleton**: In functional programming, global state is discouraged. A singleton either becomes irrelevant or is replaced by passing a reference to a function or a persistent data structure.
- **Strategy**: This is often just passing around higher-order functions. The pattern is almost trivial, so you rarely need a "class" to represent the strategy.
- **Iterator**: FP uses enumerables, streams, or lazy sequences (like Haskell's infinite lists). The notion of an imperative iterator is replaced by higher-order functions (map, filter, reduce).

10.3.2 New or Hybrid Patterns

1. **Monadic Pipelines**: Haskell popularized the concept of **monads**, which generalize

computations that produce side effects or manage contexts (like Maybe, Either, or IO). In an OOP sense, monads can be seen as a pattern for chaining and composition—similar to a "Fluent" approach but with guaranteed constraints.

2. **Function Composition**: Instead of a **Decorator**, FP might rely on function composition to add extra behavior. A function f is composed with g to produce g∘f. This can replicate aspects of the decorator pattern with less overhead.

3. **Lens/Prism**: In purely functional languages with immutable data structures, the notion of "lenses" emerges to read or update nested fields without mutating the original object. Some might consider "Lens" a design pattern or structural mechanism unique to FP.

Diagram: Functional Composition vs. Decorator

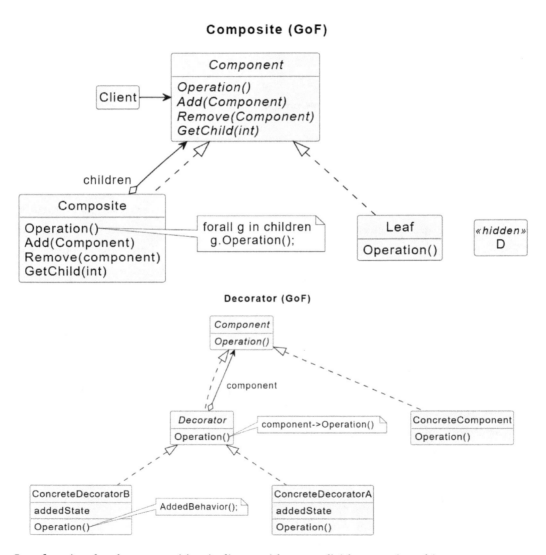

In a functional style, composition is direct, without explicitly wrapping objects.

10.3.3 Future Implications

As functional paradigms blend with OOP in mainstream languages (like Kotlin, Swift, JavaScript), we might see more hybrid patterns:

- **F(O)O-P** Patterns******: Patterns that incorporate the best of objects (encapsulation, clear layering) and pure functions (immutability, composability).
- **Effect Systems**: Next-generation typed functional languages might introduce patterns for controlling side effects, concurrency, or state changes, effectively bridging domain logic with purely functional constraints.

Thus, the future may see a redefinition or re-labeling of "design patterns" that revolve around function composition, partial application, or algebraic data types, allowing for new structures that solve recurring functional problems.

10.4 Edge Computing and IoT

Edge computing and **Internet of Things (IoT)** introduce new constraints:
- **Resource limitations**: devices with minimal CPU, memory, or battery.
- **Network intermittency**: devices might go offline or suffer high latency.
- **Geographically distributed**: thousands or millions of devices, each needing consistent patterns for data collection, updates, or local decision-making.

10.4.1 Patterns for Offline Tolerance and Synchronization

- **Offline Observer**: Traditional observer relies on immediate event dispatch. In IoT, an "offline observer" might queue events locally, synchronizing once connectivity is restored. This extends the **Observer** pattern with local caching or journaling.
- **Command with Deferred Execution**: An IoT device might queue commands from a server until it is back online. This approach merges the **Command** pattern with a "retry-on-connect" mechanism, ensuring reliability under intermittent conditions.

10.4.2 Micro Orchestration Patterns

At the edge, each device might run a small orchestrator that decides how to respond to local sensor data or triggers. Patterns like **Strategy** or **State** can define how a device transitions among "idle," "active," or "fault" states, or picks a data compression strategy based on battery levels. Meanwhile, a **Mediator** might coordinate multiple sensor modules on a single device.

Diagram: Edge Device State Transitions

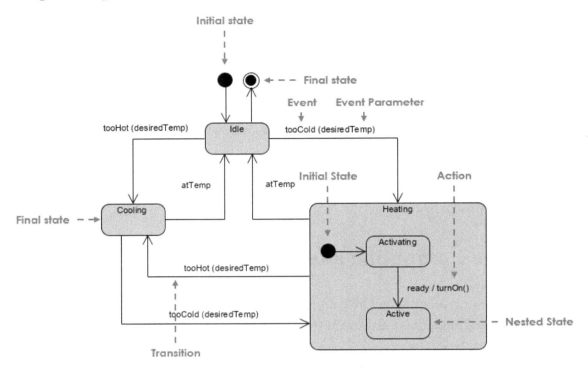

10.4.3 Security and Distribution

Edge computing heightens security concerns. Patterns like **Proxy** might help isolate device logic from direct external calls, ensuring all traffic goes through a secure gateway. Alternatively, a device might run an **Adapter** that translates local protocols (like MQTT) into an internal format for server consumption. As IoT scales, these patterns help keep the entire system maintainable, upgradable, and secure.

10.5 Patterns in Quantum Computing (Speculative Outlook)

Quantum computing is still nascent, but as it matures, we may face an entirely new approach to algorithm design—**quantum algorithms** differ drastically from classical ones, focusing on superposition, entanglement, and measurement. While it might seem far-fetched to speak of "design patterns" in quantum computing, we can speculate on possible parallels:

10.5.1 High-Level Patterns in Hybrid Classical-Quantum Systems

Most quantum solutions revolve around a classical "driver" that orchestrates quantum circuits or queries. We might see patterns such as:

- **Circuit Factory**: A specialized factory that constructs quantum circuits for different problem instances. Each "product" is a circuit prepped for gate operations.
- **Observer** (Measurement)**: The quantum system remains in superposition until a measurement collapses the state. We might define an observer-like pattern that triggers classical post-processing once a measurement event occurs.

10.5.2 Abstraction Patterns

Quantum algorithms revolve around gates (like H, CNOT, T, etc.) applied to qubits. Creating a maintainable structure for these gates might require patterns:

- **Decorator** for Gate Compositions**: One could wrap a base gate with additional transformations, though the complexity of quantum operations might require a new vocabulary.
- **Composite**: Group multiple gates or sub-circuits into a composite circuit that can be manipulated as a single object.

While it's speculative, the principle that design patterns help abstract and reapply solutions to recurring structural or interaction problems remains. As quantum computing matures, it will likely require a new library of patterns, bridging classical orchestrations with quantum operations.

10.6 Evolving Patterns for Concurrency and Parallelism

Modern CPUs are shipping with ever-increasing core counts, and distributed HPC (High-Performance Computing) or GPU-based clusters are mainstream. Traditional concurrency solutions—threads, locks, event loops—are no longer sufficient for advanced parallel workloads. We can foresee patterns that structure concurrency more robustly:

10.6.1 Actor Model

While the **Actor Model** is not a "Gang of Four" pattern, it's widely seen as a concurrency design pattern: each actor is a self-contained object with a mailbox, reacting to messages. This pattern ensures isolation and concurrency at scale. In the future, we might see:

- **Actor Decorators**: Wrappers around actors that provide logging, caching, or security checks without changing the actor's core logic.
- **Supervisor Trees**: A structural approach (akin to **Composite**) where a root actor supervises child actors, each child can supervise sub-children, forming a tree of responsibilities.

10.6.2 Dataflow Patterns

In parallel or stream-based computing, data flows through a network of transformations. This resembles **Pipes and Filters**, but with more advanced scheduling or partitioning. We might see new patterns that define how data streams are chunked, distributed, and merged:

- **Partition-Mapper-Reducer**: A specialized pattern formalizing how large data sets are split, processed in parallel, then combined. Not unlike MapReduce, but extended to flexible dataflow frameworks.

- **Windowing Observers**: In streaming analytics, an "observer" might only react to data in a certain time window. This merges observer concepts with time-based windows, creating a new structural pattern for real-time analytics.

Diagram: Dataflow Pipeline with Advanced Patterns

10.6.3 Formal Verification Patterns

As concurrency complexities mount, formal methods for verifying concurrency patterns might become standard. We can envision design patterns that come with proven correctness artifacts, or frameworks that guarantee the safe composition of concurrency building blocks. Such patterns would shift from purely structural/behavioral definitions to ones with established correctness proofs or concurrency models (like linear types or session types).

10.7 Low-Code/No-Code and Patterns

Low-code and **no-code** platforms allow non-technical users to create workflows, forms, and small apps by dragging and dropping components. This might seem antithetical to code-based design patterns, but as these solutions become more complex, the same architectural issues emerge: duplication, tangled logic, difficult changes. Patterns can:

1. **Inspire** the platform's "blocks" or "templates," representing a pattern at a higher abstraction. For instance, a no-code tool might have a "Approval Chain" block implementing a **Chain of Responsibility** for approvals, configurable by drag-and-drop.

2. **Guide** best practices within the platform: A user might design a multi-step workflow that resonates with a known pattern (like **Command** for undoable steps, or **Observer** for reactive updates) but expressed visually rather than textually.

10.7.1 Hybrid Developer Experiences

Teams might combine no-code front-end forms with a robust code-based back-end. Patterns bridging the two worlds could appear:

- **API Facade**: A no-code front end interacts with an internal **Facade** that simplifies service calls.
- **State Machines**: A no-code tool might define states and transitions for user journeys, effectively implementing a **State** pattern under the hood.

As no-code platforms evolve to handle larger, more mission-critical tasks, design patterns will remain essential to keep them from devolving into unmanageable "spaghetti diagrams." We can anticipate future expansions where a no-code platform explicitly references known patterns to shape how a user drags logic blocks or sets event triggers.

10.8 Patterns as a Teaching Tool and Collaboration Medium

Design patterns have long been used to teach software architecture. In the future, we may see deeper expansions:

10.8.1 Mixed Reality and Visual Pattern Editors

Imagine an IDE that visually overlays UML-like diagrams, letting developers drag lines between classes, methods, or modules to define pattern relationships. This environment could automatically generate or maintain the corresponding code stubs or references. We might have:

- **"Pattern Wizard"**: An interactive guide that steps you through implementing a pattern, verifying that your code adheres to the correct structure.
- **AR/VR-based Collaboration**: Remote teams might gather in a virtual space, see the architecture as 3D shapes, and apply patterns by rearranging nodes or "attaching" decorators in a visually tangible manner.

10.8.2 Domain Experts and Patterns

As domain-driven design gains momentum, we see domain experts more directly shaping the software. Patterns could be described in domain language, bridging the conceptual gap. For instance, an expert might define a "ApprovalFlow pattern" that is a specialized version of **Chain of Responsibility**. Code is generated or refined automatically, ensuring the domain remains front-and-center.

10.8.3 Patterns in Education

Beyond advanced IDE features, patterns remain a powerful tool for teaching novices. In the future, we might see more creative, interactive tutorials or puzzle-like learning platforms that show incomplete code with placeholders for pattern components. By solving these "pattern puzzles," students internalize the structure of patterns. Coupled with AI-driven feedback, the environment can adapt challenges to each learner's skill level, reinforcing pattern knowledge.

10.9 Synergy with Emerging Technologies

We've touched on some advanced fields, but the technology landscape is ever-shifting. The unifying theme is that design patterns provide stable conceptual frameworks even as the underlying paradigms shift.

10.9.1 Blockchain and Decentralized Systems

Blockchain solutions or decentralized networks might adapt patterns around consensus, data immutability, and trust. For example:

- **Proxy** or **Mediator** for bridging on-chain logic with off-chain oracles.
- **Observer** for event watchers that react to new blocks or transactions in real time.
- **Memento** for state snapshots across distributed ledgers (though blockchains themselves store a full transaction history, a variant of Memento might handle ephemeral off-chain state).

10.9.2 Extended Reality (XR) and Gaming

As XR and VR become mainstream, multi-user, immersive experiences require robust patterns for synchronization and user state updates:

- **Mediator** for managing interactions among virtual objects in a shared scene.
- **Decorator** or **Flyweight** to handle large numbers of similar 3D assets efficiently, controlling memory usage in VR.
- **State** for AR-based user flows or "modes" (navigating, scanning environment, placing virtual objects).

10.9.3 Collaborative AI Tools

Generative AI that writes or refactors code is likely to grow more integrated into the developer workflow. Patterns can serve as **knowledge anchors** for these tools, letting them propose consistent, tested designs rather than ad-hoc logic. This synergy might standardize code structure in large, multi-developer projects, further elevating the importance of pattern-based guidelines.

Diagram: Patterns Bridging AI, Cloud, and IoT

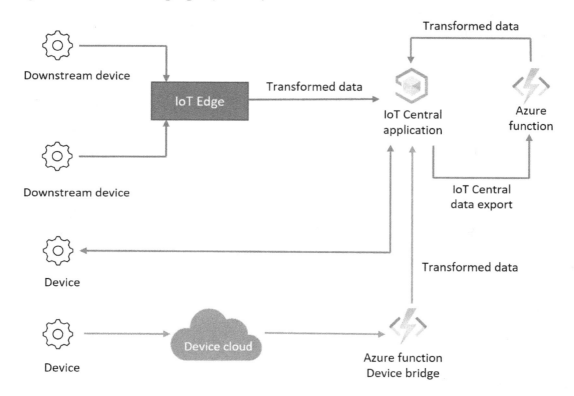

10.10 Timeless Principles and the Road Ahead

Despite all these future-oriented predictions, the core essence of design patterns remains rooted in **timeless** principles:

1. **Separation of Concerns**: Ensuring that distinct parts of the system handle distinct responsibilities.

2. **Loosely Coupled Components**: Minimizing direct dependencies so pieces can change or scale independently.

3. **Modular, Reusable Solutions**: Patterns capture solutions that can be transplanted or adapted across projects.

4. **Human-Centric Communication**: Patterns let developers quickly discuss and debate design choices at a higher level than raw code.

As the boundaries of software expand—whether it's cloud-native, quantum computations, or AI-driven solutions—these principles stay relevant. Patterns are not static artifacts but living design heuristics that can be recast or extended to match new paradigms.

10.10.1 Patterns as Evolving Heuristics

Each generation of developers re-discovers or re-invents certain patterns when confronting new problems. For instance, concurrency patterns blossomed once multicore CPUs became standard. We can expect new waves of pattern definitions or formalizations as machine learning, serverless, and edge computing become standard. The "Gang of Four" patterns might remain the backbone, but we'll see new patterns or sub-patterns that help unify event streams, ephemeral resources, or partial data states.

10.10.2 Patterns Across Disciplines

Another possible frontier is more explicit cross-domain synergy. For instance, data scientists or UX designers might define "patterns" for data transformations or user flows that parallel software design patterns at the code level. The future could see integrated "meta-patterns" that unify domain logic, user experience, and system architecture under a consistent approach to problem-solving.

www.ingramcontent.com/pod-product-compliance
Lightning Source LLC
LaVergne TN
LVHW080116070326
832902LV00015B/2621